ROAD TO
AIR AMERICA

ROAD TO AIR AMERICA

Breaking the Right Wing Stranglehold on Our Nation's Air Waves

SHELDON DROBNY

Donated By:
Sheldon & Anita Drobny

SelectBooks, Inc.

Road to Air America: Breaking the Right Wing Stranglehold on Our Nation's Airwaves

©2004 Anita Drobny

This edition published by SelectBooks, Inc.
For information address SelectBooks, Inc., One Union Square West, New York, New York 10003

First Edition

ISBN 1-59079-065-0

Library of Congress Cataloging-in-Publication Data
Drobny, Sheldon.
  Road to Air America : breaking the right wing stranglehold on our nation's air waves / Sheldon Drobny.-- 1st ed.
    p. cm.
  ISBN 1-59079-065-0 (hardcover : alk. paper)
  1. Radio in politics--United States. 2. Air America Radio--History. 3. Radio broadcasting--United States--History--20th century. 4. Right and left
(Political science)   I. Title.
HE8697.85.U6D76 2004
384.54'55'0973--dc22
                          2004018150

Manufactured in the United States of America

10 9 8 7 6 5 4 3 2

Dedicated to the everlasting spirit of my father, Charles Drobny
and the nurturing wisdom of my wife, earth mother Anita

Contents

Acknowledgements   *ix*

Introduction   *xi*

1   On the Air   1

2   Dreams and Nightmares Come True   5

3   Tuned In, Turned Off   9

4   Back to Roots   15

5   Eisenhower's Warning   19

6   The Wake Up Call   25

7   Getting Connected   33

8   Lost History   39

9   In Business   45

10   Planning the Road Show   49

11   Launch Number One   53

12   On Our Way   59

13   The Psychology of Money   65

14   Meet the Radio Skeptics   71

15 Just Say Yes   77

16 Air America Takes Off   81

17 In the Spotlight   85

18 The Mad Dash   91

19 First, the Good News   97

20 Conference Room Confidential   101

21 Facing the Future   105

Postscript   111

Appendix A   115

Appendix B   121

Appendix C   131

Glossary of New Orwellian Terms   141

Acknowledgments

There are many people who deserve thanks for helping to get Air America Radio off the ground. I thank all of you for your efforts—those who are part of the story told here, and those who I did not mention by name. I am grateful to you for your commitment and participation.

I also thank my father Charles for imparting to me a lifetime of experiences and readings that allowed me to know true history and to be passionate about the cause of the people. I also want to express my everlasting love for my wife Anita, and thank her for putting up with this passion for over twenty-five years.

The support we got from the Clintons and Gores was especially helpful to our cause. I am deeply grateful. Their efforts were instrumental in helping to make the Air America project happen. I especially want to thank Tony Rodham, who behind the scenes, gave everything he had to make Air America Radio a success. He is a terrific guy and dedicated to the cause.

Congresswoman Jan Schakowsky and her husband and political advisor Bob Creamer gave us great advice and helped to energize our passion to continue the project. Mike Lux and his Progressive Donor Network were terrific. Bob Borosage from Take Back America was a great support and served on our original board of advisors.

There are many people in radio I must thank, but the people I am most grateful to are Jon Sinton and Mike Malloy. I am so glad they are both still a part of Air America. Jon is a terrific radio executive and committed to his vision; he has been a part of Air America Radio from the start. Mike Malloy is the experienced workhorse of liberal talk radio. His frustrations about the state of talk radio helped to convince us that there was a market out there. At last, he is now a regular on The Air America Radio network.

I am grateful to the board of directors of Air America Radio who helped to save this wonderful project. They are great people, and they put this project ahead of almost everything.

A special thank-you goes to all the "black listed" independent investigative reporters who are not working today because of their dedication. Bob Parry was an investigative reporter for the AP who helped uncover the Iran/Contra affair. It was my pleasure to meet him and engage him in the attempt to fund independent investigative reporting with the formation of the Fourth Estate Society.

John Loftus, who wrote *The Secret War Against The Jews,* was an inspiration to me for his work about exposing those American industrialists who aided the Nazis. He discovered this information while he was trying to prosecute them when he was with The Justice Department.

Thanks to Julie Schwartzman for helping me to write my first book. I learned a lot from her about writing a book in lightening speed. I would also like to thank Bill Gladstone for helping me to get *Road to Air America* published, and Joanna Posner for interviewing people and giving me additional material to write some of the chapters. Also thanks to Carolyn Kay for her help with editing.

Finally, I would like to thank Thom Hartmann, who wrote the article called "Talking Back to Talk Radio." His advice to us about the wide open market has been invaluable. Thom is now a successful syndicated liberal talk show host in his own right.

All of you have been with me on the Road to Air America.

Introduction

This is the story of a major media rollout in this country. It's a story you don't hear often these days; corporate ownership of media and the high cost of entering the market have made it almost impossible to bring a new voice to American media. Not only did we face huge financial challenges, we faced relentless skepticism from the radio establishment. As Jon Sinton, current President of Air America Radio puts it, "Everybody said it couldn't be done. It's done."

When we started in May 2002, Anita and I did not foresee how difficult and treacherous the journey would be. I am grateful that we did not know, since otherwise we might not have tried to launch the first liberal talk radio network in the country.

Anita and I have been actively involved in political and philanthropic causes all our adult lives. It has been only in the past ten years that we had the wherewithal to donate significant sums of money to those causes. We were very proud of our grant to the University of Illinois Jewish Studies Program in 1997, the largest of its kind for any state supported university. We were pleased and honored to be involved in political causes with some of the most powerful and influential people in this country. We had hoped that we, the Drobnys, could help make a difference in the world. We genuinely wanted to help improve the human condition—no small ambition. However, we soon found out that the most powerful people seemed to be helpless about changing the state of affairs in this country, even with all their alleged power and money. We soon found out why.

Since the end of World War II, this country has become the most corporate-dominated and influenced nation in history. The great experiment that our founders had foreseen has been taken hostage by insidious and powerful multinational companies with the willing aid of their government. We have gone from a democratic culture to an industrial corporate oligarchy. And the major reason for this most recent rise of corporate power has been the power of the corporate-owned press who use the media to further their interests.

Calvin Coolidge is famous for saying: "The chief business of the American people is business," which has become a mantra for industry's unchecked enthusiasm for the free market. However no one quotes his words prior to this part of the speech in which he says, "There does not seem to be cause for alarm in the dual relationship of the press to the public, whereby it is on one side a purveyor of information and opinion and on the other side a purely business enterprise." Coolidge was not worried because he believed the press—and business in general—had a responsibility to be reliable, enlightening, and loyal to the vision of the American nation, and he trusted in the media's ability to live up to that responsibility.

Far from believing business was synonymous with pure materialism, Coolidge also said in that famous speech, "The accumulation of wealth cannot be justified as the chief end of existence." He believed American newspapers were "particularly representative of this practical idealism of our people."

How disappointed he would be if he could see where his misplaced trust has led us. Today the corporate media sells more advertising and makes more money than any one ever believed possible, yet offers less and less enlightenment. The media, increasingly, seems to be at the beck and call of the powerful and elite. The only idealism found in today's conglomerates seems to be in the accumulation of profits. This is why local news is little more than weather, sports, and murder; why investigative journalism and serious content is so rare; why debased scandal takes up pages of print, while genuine issues get little coverage. Real news is not profitable. Cheap entertainment is.

Serious debate, meaningful content, and responsible reporting is an increasing rarity in media today. We founded Air America Radio in order to create a place for real discourse and alternative news in America. Coolidge—rightly or wrongly—may be associated with supporting the predatory nature of big business. But in founding Air America Radio we started with a different insight from the Vermont-born President: "Prosperity is only an instrument to be used, not a deity to be worshiped."

We realized that the only way to change the status quo of profit worship was to take action ourselves, to take back control of the media anyway we could—even if it meant starting our own network. That's how the Air America story began.

ROAD TO
AIR AMERICA

1

On the Air

At twelve noon, a rocking guitar riff goes out over the AM radio airwaves, followed by the voice of Al Franken. In a deep tone, full of classic rock radio spirit, he announces, "It's Wednesday, August 12, and the first hour of the Al Franken show begins…" Franken's Grateful Dead theme song kicks in, as he continues, energetically announcing the day's show's guests, as well as the program's special segments—bits with names like the "Oy, Oy, Oy Show," or a visit with the show's "Resident Dittohead." If it all gives you the feeling that a good time is on the way, you won't be disappointed. The most popular show on Air America—the country's first liberal radio network—is on the air.

Sitting across from Al is Franken in the New York City studios of Air America, is Franken's sidekick, Katherine Lanpher. She's crisp and precise, a perfect complement to Franken's easygoing radio persona. Every day from noon to three o' clock Franken and Lanpher spend three hours interviewing political figures and journalists, taking calls, and performing sharp political satire. Most of it is against a background of liberal indignation at the almost endless examples of Republican deception, duplicity, and mismanagement. As Franken says, "If you're feeling down after a day of Republican lies, we're here to help."

As a radio host, Franken has mastered the art of sounding genial and happy, even as he's delivering a ruthless account of the latest Bush Administration boondoggle. Franken's balancing act —easy-to-listen-to, razor sharp political commentary—is propelling him up the ratings.

Today's guests are Richard Ben-Veniste, one of the ten commissioners on the 9/11 Commission. Later, former Senator Gary Hart will stop by to talk about why no one in the Bush Administration heeded his warning of a catastrophic terrorism attack, published a full year before September 11, 2001, in the report by the Hart–Rudman Commission. They'll talk about democracy, civic virtue, and the common good; this is comedy with content.

Somewhere in the first hour of the show, Franken will do his signature skewering of Rush Limbaugh, discrediting Limbaugh by playing actual clips of his show, then contrasting them with facts, data, and sound bites of real speeches, proving—yet again—that Rush is "pulling stuff out of his butt," as Franken describes it.

On today's show, Franken, Lanpher, and their guests will discuss the Medicare Bill, the war in Iraq, local senate races, Republican "ethics waivers," competing Swift Boat claims, and Halliburton, with time left over to fit in his game show, *Wait, Wait, Don't Lie To Me.*

Hilarious as it is informative, *Wait, Wait, Don't Lie to Me,* has callers guessing whether a Republican statement is "a lie, weasel words, or the truth." The subject is usually something from Rush, Bill O' Reilly, Sean Hannity or another Republican spokesperson. On a typical weekday, Air America will be heard in 31 different markets, a number that has been growing steadily week by week. It appears Franken's show has gotten a foothold in talk radio, and is closing in on the competition in the same time slot—Rush Limbaugh. Air America is the number one station in Portland, Oregon, and is the most listened to audio stream on the internet. For a network broadcasting only six months, it's a start.

Says Jon Sinton, President of Air America, "Before we had an idea. Now we have a business that proves itself every day by the fabulous guests, the spreading distribution, and the growing listener base."

After Franken's show, Randi Rhodes will take over with a funny and scathing show that can best be summed up as a firestorm; Rhodes has no patience for deception, whether from a pundit, a politico or a phone caller. She ruthlessly critiques anything that falls within her radar. It's a comedy blitz that goes on for four high energy hours.

Rhodes has joined Air America from South Florida where she hosted one of the most popular talk radio shows in the region, beating out Air America's dark inspiration, Rush Limbaugh, in the ratings. Later in the evening, listeners can hear Air America's latest addition, Mike Malloy, who joins the rest of the day's line up— radio veteran Mike Riley and Mike Maron with *Morning Sedition,* and actress and activist Janeane Garofalo with Sam Seder on *Majority Report.* There's also a hearty, hardcore mix of politics and comedy every morning with Lizz Winstead, co-creator of *The Daily Show,* Chuck D, founder of the band Public Enemy, and Rachel Maddow on *Unfiltered.* It's turning into one of the most entertaining radio lineups around.

Talent and good content guarantee nothing nowadays, but Air America, the country's first liberal radio network, is busy and broadcasting. People seem to be listening, which is not what the radio establishment predicted would happen.

2

Dreams and Nightmares Come True

March 31, 2004, is the day Air America Radio first went on the air. It started broadcasting in three major markets: New York, Chicago, and Los Angeles. It was not just a syndicated program or two, but a full 24 hour day of broadcasting. In addition, a few affiliates came on board in smaller cities along with two satellite radio stations. It was an accomplishment. My wife Anita and I had started something two years earlier that was now a reality.

Tears streamed down Anita's face. "I can't believe," she said, "I just can't believe it." For Anita, it was like having a baby with a 24 month gestation period. But there was a problem. This was no longer our company, and we were not a part of the opening festivities. We had sold the forerunner of Air America Radio— AnShell Media—to a group of radio entrepreneurs the previous November.

The group—for legal reasons, we'll call them "The Buyers" from now on—took over all the operations of AnShell Media and its management team, as well as our relationships with talent like Al Franken and Janeane Garofalo. Anita and I had laid the ground work for the organization, but we could not get the funding needed to do justice to the enterprise. The Buyers had both the experience and money necessary to complete the job.

We turned over the company to them with the agreement that they would get Air America Radio on the air. We also had an agreement that when The Buyers had gotten Air America Radio on in three major markets, AnShell was entitled to a milestone payment of at least $750,000. Until that point, we deferred all other payment. The Buyers paid nothing up front, but agreed to use their own money. They would fundraise and finance Air America's operations. There were other milestone payments we believed were coming to us, but the important thing was that Air America Radio was broadcasting.

Since we had sold the company, as noted, opening day for Air America Radio did not include us. There had been a gala celebration the previous evening at the Maritime Hotel in New York City. We were not there or even mentioned. When we sold AnShell media, it was agreed that Anita and I would be given founder recognition and Anita would be chairperson of the advisory board for Air America. Not only was Anita not made chairperson of the advisory board, but any contact between Air America staff and Anita and me was prohibited by The Buyers. Although we thought it was equivalent to George and Martha Washington being written out of American history, Anita and I accepted the fact that we would be out of the loop. Nothing could take away from us the fact that we got Air America Radio started.

The next day, with Air America officially on the air in three markets, I wrote an email to The Buyers informing them that our milestone payment of $750,000 was due as per our agreement. I got no answer. After a couple of days, I called Javier Saade, my former partner in the Paradigm Group, a venture capital firm of which Anita and I are the founders. Javier had been with us almost from the beginning. He had worked on the original business plan for AnShell Media in September of 2002, and had been instrumental in putting together the necessary information for presentation to prospective investors. Once AnShell had been acquired, Javier joined the Air America corporate team as its CFO.

I felt perfectly comfortable calling Javier to find out whether Air America intended to pay us. Again, I got no answer from Javier. Finally I called Javier and left a voice mail message that was extremely animated, to say the least. Ten minutes later I got a response. Poor Javier was caught in the middle. He said he could not talk about this because he had been instructed not to talk to me or Anita. Javier said he had to go. It appeared I would need to turn this over to my attorney.

Anita and I are fortunate to have a terrific attorney, Rick Bernthal of Latham and Watkins. He has been our attorney since we formed AnShell Media, and he also reviewed the asset purchase agreement for the transfer of assets from AnShell to Radio Free America, the company The Buyers formed to operate Air America Radio. Rick suggested that we give them another week to respond to the payment requests before he took any action. We all agreed to wait.

3

Tuned In, Turned Off

Even though I knew that we had a good legal position, I began to suspect that we had a serious problem—one that our attorney could not resolve with just a phone call. I had a feeling the reason we weren't paid was because Air America Radio was out of money, even though it had only been on the air a few days.

It has been my experience as a venture capitalist that people who withhold payments do so because they have no choice. The prospects for payment were gloomy. More importantly, I began to be concerned about the survival of Air America Radio itself. The Buyers had been running the show for five months now, and I wondered how much longer they could last. It was early April 2004.

The following week, Anita and I were in DC having a meeting with David Brock about a new project to support independent investigative reporting, called the Fourth Estate Society. David Brock is a former conservative who wrote articles about Paula Jones for *The American Spectator,* a right wing publication that gave voice to many of those who wished to destroy the Clinton Presidency. He has since written two books about how dishonest and corrupt his former employers had been. The Fourth Estate Society is a non-profit entity designed to help journalists do the kind of investigative reporting that been slowly disappearing since the major media companies started to dominate the dissemination of information in the U.S.

David Brock was excited about the project and offered to help us. Anita and I were having lunch with David when I got a call from my brother, Irving. He told me the Chicago station broadcasting Air America Radio was now broadcasting in Spanish. I laughed and said to him perhaps AAR had decided our target audience was Spanish speaking. At first I did not believe him, but ten minutes later I got a call from John Cook of *The Chicago Tribune.* He asked me if I knew anything about why Air America Radio was shut down in Chicago and Los Angeles. I did not have a clue. Then I remembered my earlier suspicion: Air America's well had indeed run dry. They were out of money.

Suddenly we found ourselves in the middle of a crisis that was almost funny in spite of its negative impact. It appeared—not just to Anita and me but to the whole world—that Air America was in big trouble. Behind the scenes it seemed like the Keystone Cops were running Air America Radio. Everyone at Air America scrambling and bumping into each other to trying to find the root of the financial problems that had shut down the station in Chicago and Los Angeles. It was crisis management at its worst.

I was afraid if this news got out the right wing would have a field day. Anita called David Goodfriend, the general counsel for Air America Radio, to ask him what was happening. David told Anita that apparently Air America had stopped payment on a check written to the LA and Chicago station owner. I took the phone from Anita and asked David about the wisdom of stopping payment on a check to the company that controls the proverbial broadcast switch. I told him I thought stopping payment on the check was stupid, comparable to stopping payment on the company that has you on a life support machine. You might be right, but the end result would be you were dead. Funny what kind of foolish excuses people make when they're desperate.

The next day, Air America Radio obtained a temporary court order to get it back on the air in Chicago. Even though I was no longer a part of Air America's operations, I wanted to know what was going on. I got in touch with one of Air America's officers, Doug Kreeger. Doug was Executive Vice President and a significant investor in both AnShell and Air America. Doug, Anita, and I stayed in constant contact over the next couple of weeks, as the upper levels of Air America's management began to reveal the problems and cash flow crisis.

Everything finally collapsed on May 5, 2004, when we got a call from Doug Kreeger telling us that the company was hopelessly in debt. He asked that Anita and I come to New York for an emergency meeting of the other investors in Air America Radio. We got on the next flight to New York City.

We arrived in New York that same day and were escorted to a conference room at the offices of Air America Radio. The room was crowded with investors and attorneys. There were also people on a conference call as part of the meeting. The room was steaming and so were the people. Had we come this far just to shut down only a month after launching?

The good news was that the investment group was composed of people who wanted Air America Radio to survive, and who were wealthy enough to do something about it. Before we sold the company to The Buyers, Anita and I were the only investors. Now we had real partners who would not let Air America go down—if someone could figure out how to reorganize.

Anita and I had three decades of experience behind us in financial workouts, including situations much like this one. The Buyers were in default of their contract, and the company was returning to our hands. Before we got to New York we had discussed the basis of a plan to reorganize Air America Radio into a clean company with as few encumbrances as possible. We discussed this workout plan on the flight to New York, something we had done many times before for companies faced with similar financial difficulties.

Anita and I, along with our lawyers, Rick Bernthal and Michael Schlesinger, formed a new entity to operate Air America. We arranged to reorganize the company, while retaining the right to use the trade name. We began the process of converting lemons into lemonade.

The broadcasting staff of Air America Radio did not miss a beat. They stayed on the job and on the air. Everyone was on board with our recovery plan, both employees and talent. Al Franken, our most recognized talent, was wonderful in his leadership role, and during the company's worst moments he kept his staff calm, focused, and patient, giving us the opportunity to get things under control. The support of both talent and staff allowed us to recover from Air America's past sins; we reorganized, provided interim funding and as of this writing, have commitments for all the capital we need.

In addition, our Arbitron ratings were terrific in New York and the rest of the country. The web site has been setting records with their streaming internet broadcasts estimated to be in the range of 2,000,000 hits per week, and averaging around forty-five minutes each.

It seemed the radio analysts had been wrong. Before Air America Radio even went on the air, they had pronounced it dead. The radio establishment had believed the propaganda the right wing was feeding the mainstream media, that there is no market for progressive radio.

It turns out that not only is there a market for liberal radio, but these consumers are the best audience for advertisers, as was reported in a recent article by John Cook in *The Chicago Tribune.* Cook reported that the quality of our audience in the young adult category was far superior to those in right wing talk radio.

To the radio establishment it might look like the liberal consumer of information appeared out of nowhere. But we always believed they were there, and Air America has figured out how to reach them.

Out of the ashes, Air America Radio is alive and well, and getting noticed by radio station owners who have underperforming stations and are looking for alternatives to right wing radio. They, like us, realize that there are two talk radio markets, not just one.

Anita and I, both children of immigrant parents, had no experience whatever in radio. We had an idea that we thought was obvious. But, as they say, there is nothing as invisible as the obvious.

4

Back to the Roots

I was fortunate to have a father who was an avid reader and political junky. He was also a die-hard Chicago Cub fan and unfortunately never lived to see them win a World Series. But he did see a lot of things change for the worse in this country since he came to America with his family in 1921 at the age of fifteen.

My father, Charles Drobny, grew up in a small Polish town called Nova Miasto, sixty kilometers north of Warsaw. At that time, Poland was occupied by Czarist Russia and he lived through the many injustices and pogroms of the type described by Sholom Aleichem's character Tevya in *Fiddler on the Roof*. The plight of the Jews in his home country caused my father to become an active member of the Socialist Workers Movement during that time. For the Jews of that era, that was the only movement in which they were fully embraced. This relief from anti-Semitism is one of the reasons why so many Jews of that era were true believers in the socialist movement: it was their first taste of justice.

Dad told me many stories about his past and the injustices he had faced as a child. During World War I he remembered how the Jews of his town were more afraid of their own army than the invading Germans. The Germans during World War I were not

nearly as anti-Semitic as the Russians. When the Germans occupied Nova Miasto, the Jews came out from hiding, and the
German soldiers gave him and the other children chocolates and
candy. When the Russian soldiers returned, the Jews went back
into hiding. It was a paradox to him that one should be afraid of
one's own country's army, and he wanted to express this paradox
to his children.

He was also a witness to events in history that were never fully
reported in the U.S. press. Many of these events of the first half of
the twentieth century should have been reported for the public
interest. However, as he used to say, the media does not always serve
the public interest. Or, as he put it, not pulling any punches, "the
newspapers are run by a bunch of greedy, lying bastards."

The corporate media will even help change history to serve its
own purposes. The media today is doing it even more than in the
times in which my father lived. Whether it's the war in Iraq, the
economy, or Homeland Security, many Americans feel that the corporate media is not giving them the full story. It was our desire to
ensure, with the creation of Air America Radio, the public does not
let them get away with this much longer.

My father married Sarah Lopata in 1936 and they had three sons:
Irving, Arnold, and me, Sheldon. I was the youngest of the three.
We grew up in on the West Side of Chicago in a small one bedroom
apartment. We kids all slept in the bedroom and our parents slept
in a Murphy bed in the living room. We all shared one bathroom
and it was chaos getting ready for school in the morning. My father
had a small fruit store in the neighborhood with his brother as his
partner. The neighborhood started to deteriorate in the early '50s
but my dad was able to expand his fruit store into a grocery store.
By 1953 my struggling Socialist father became a successful capitalist, which gave our family the opportunity to move into our own
home in a beautiful neighborhood on the northwest side of Chicago.
I was eight years old at the time. Our family had just entered the
middle class.

We were indoctrinated with Dad's socialist values and many of his views. In spite of working almost constantly—he spent seven days a week at the store—he would find time to talk to his kids. It might be when he got home for dinner, or on Sunday afternoons when the store was only opened for half a day. Once he got going, there was no stopping him and we would listen to his stories for hours at a time.

Like many idealistic Jews of that era, my father was optimistic about the promise of socialism, but blind to the fact that Stalin was an oppressive dictator. He had observed that Hitler was the greater threat and told us many stories about how the Western powers were willing to appease Hitler because of his anti-communist policy. He constantly criticized our leaders for allowing the corporate interests of our country to help rearm Germany. He believed the profiteering in the armaments industry of this country helped to build up Hitler's Germany—a scandal that has still not been fully exposed in this country.

He was painfully aware that, without money or influence, he did not have the means or power to make any real changes in the government, and so he would constantly curse the politicians he hated. I remember when he wished that Senator McCarthy would die, and within a few months he did die. In the mind of a ten year old kid, that was pretty impressive. Dad was known for his famous curses to politicians he hated. He wished a cancer on John Foster Dulles and sure enough, Dulles died of cancer shortly after that. In 1968 I asked Dad if he wished a cancer on the great segregationist George Wallace of Alabama. Dad said cancer was too good for him and wished for him to be paralyzed. Sure enough, within a month, Wallace was shot and became paralyzed for life. Now that to me was a powerful man.

Despite the fact that my father seemed to possess the power to place curses on people, he was frustrated by the fact that he could not influence any real changes in government. Although he was not a member of any political organization, he read many books about politics and read a daily Yiddish language socialist newspaper called *The Morning Freiheit. The Morning Freiheit* was a popular daily founded by the Jewish wing of the American Communist Party.

The business of war was something addressed by Eisenhower in his farewell address. His vision of the military-industrial complex is worse than anyone ever dreamed it would be. For example, Eisenhower could not have foreseen that General Electric, one of the big providers of the armaments industry, now owns NBC, an entertainment industry powerhouse. How can corporate-owned media be objective about the news when some of that news will damage its own interests? What picture of the world could you expect NBC to report, given this conflict of interest? These are the questions my father would have asked, were he around today, and they're the questions I ask today. In my opinion, these are the questions that should be raised by our political leaders.

Unfortunately, they are paralyzed not only by the power of money, but by the power of the very media they should be critiquing.

5

Eisenhower's Warning

Whether because of the accounts my father passed along to me, or because of my own experience, the power of the media has always fascinated me. I became an avid follower of the machinations of media companies and corporations in general, and of their growing and unchecked power.

I have read contemporary writings by noted authors and historians, as well as lesser known sources, absorbed the observations of my father, and formed my own conclusions when it comes to "the business of America." I believe large corporate interests, aided and abetted by the major media, have been responsible for reporting and writing history that suits their own interests.

I read with particular interest President Eisenhower's powerful farewell address when he warned us of the obstacles our democracy would face in the coming years. In my opinion, it was the most important and prophetic farewell speech in our history. The segment of the speech below is one that has been quoted many times. I believe few political leaders have heeded Eisenhower's warning. Eisenhower said:

> Our military organization today bears little relation to that known by any of my predecessors in peacetime, or indeed by the fighting men of World War II or Korea.

Until the latest of our world conflicts, the United States had no armaments industry. American makers of plowshares could, with time and as required, make swords as well. But now we can no longer risk emergency improvisation of national defense; we have been compelled to create a permanent armaments industry of vast proportions. Added to this, three and a half million men and women are directly engaged in the defense establishment. We annually spend on military security more than the net income of all United States corporations.

This conjunction of an immense military establishment and a large arms industry is new in the American experience. The total influence-economic, political, even spiritual—is felt in every city, every State House, every office of the Federal government. We recognize the imperative need for this development. Yet we must not fail to comprehend its grave implications. Our toil, resources and livelihood are all involved; so is the very structure of our society.

Eisenhower warned that our very liberties themselves were endangered by the combination of industrial arms manufacturers and the nation's war machine. He continued, introducing the phrase that is now part of the English Language, "In the councils of government, we must guard against the acquisition of unwarranted influence, whether sought or unsought, by the military-industrial complex. The potential for the disastrous rise of misplaced power exists and will persist."

Americans should be forever grateful for the courage it took Eisenhower to make this speech in light of the political and economic forces opposed to it. As the Supreme Commander of Allied Forces in Europe during World War II, he had seen the evolution of the immense war profiteering by American and European industrialist, starting with the buildup of Hitler's Germany.

The buildup of the military in Nazi Germany is a matter of public record. In violation of the Versailles Treaty, Germany started to rebuild its war machine in the mid-1930s, including the initiation of conscription. Under the Versailles Treaty, the German standing army was limited to 100,000. This was forbidden.

Why did the Allies stand by and let these things happen? Hitler made lucrative armaments deals with German, American, and other European industrialists. For example, recently released documents from the National Archives have disclosed that leading American industrialists including G. Roland Harriman and Prescott Bush were owners and directors of a company that did business with the Nazis. Their company was The Union Banking Corporation and its assets were frozen in 1942 under the Trading with the Enemies Act. They were hardly alone. Allegedly, companies like ITT, General Motors, Ford, Standard Oil of New Jersey, and Texaco, along with families including the Rockefellers, Fords, DuPonts, and Morgans showed their sympathies for the Nazi War movement in a variety of ways. The Rockefellers, too, were called before not one, but two senate committees to review their potential violation of the Trading with the Enemies Act.

Without the cooperation of American capitalists and other international corporations, the German rearmament could not have happened. The big prize in all this for American industrialists was the huge profits generated by such contracts. Much of this profiteering has never been exposed.

Although it was clear that, at the time, Nazis were committing genocidal acts against Jews, their political enemies, gypsies, and others, these American capitalists were motivated by profits, not humanism. Some were ideologically supportive of the Nazi regime.

American capitalists had feared the dominance of the Soviet Union and Communism ever since the 1917 Bolshevik Revolution. As part of the ruling class these industrialists had a complete abhorrence of socialism. These Western industrialists were afraid of a growing workers movement in their own countries, as well as the rise of union power. They clearly believed that the events in Russia would give rise to a worldwide workers' revolt. This is why they had no qualms about rearming Germany; as noted, Hitler was the greatest adversary of the USSR and communism in general before the War. In fact, after World War I, the U.S., Britain, and France sent armed forces to the USSR to overthrow the Bolsheviks. That intervention was not easily forgotten by the Soviet Government. The Allies' interference in the Russian civil war caused millions of Russian deaths, and helped to bring mass starvation to the country. In addition, it created an isolation of Russia and a closed society which would later lead to the rise of Stalin and a totalitarian government.

At that time, during the 1930s, the U.S. did not have a significant armaments industry, nor did the U.S. have a large standing army. Roosevelt did not initiate the draft until 1940—almost one year after the war in Europe began. When Pearl Harbor was attacked, only then did the nation truly begin the major buildup of our war machine with the help of the United States' great industrial capacity. The conversion of our industry to the buildup of armaments brought America out of the Great Depression. Fortunes were made by many during World War II, whether it was in the conversion of the automobile industry to the building of mobile military vehicles, or the transformation of the steel and chemical industries as suppliers in the war effort. In addition, a large underground economy made fortunes for those who peddled in goods that were rationed by the government.

Most Americans do not know that it was Hitler who declared war on the U.S. There was a great resistance in Wall Street circles to declaring war on Germany because of the massive economic relationship between Germany and the Wall Street profiteers. That is why Roosevelt declared war only on Japan. It was Hitler's unexpected decision to declare war on the U.S. on December 11, 1941, that put Wall Street into shock. Hitler's folly in declaring war on the U.S. was a major turning point in the world, and Germany's forcing the U.S. to enter the war in Europe was a military disaster for them. Even America's premiere capitalists began to consider Hitler a crazed menace. In December 1941 the U.S. was not really a military threat to Germany, but all that would change.

Hitler was deeply involved in a war with the Soviet Union and his armies had advanced deeply into Russia by December 1941. The Red Army had stopped Hitler's advance to Moscow. The Russian winter was becoming a problem. By declaring war on the U.S., Hitler thought that Japan would agree to attack Russia from Manchuria, and take the pressure off his troops outside of Moscow. The Japanese did not attack Russia from Manchuria. To Hitler's surprise, the Japanese were interested only in the Pacific war with the U.S.

Hitler's declaration of war on the U.S. created a problem for the Wall Street armaments industrialists who supported Hitler's military buildup. With Germany now our sworn enemy, they were faced with the unhappy task of covering up their participation in creating the most powerful armed forces in the world. How would they hide their participation?

The media was there to help. Pressures and patriotism kept much of this out of the papers. America's press ran to keep up with current events, and various political forces were used to keep corporate collusion out of the papers, as America turned its eye towards the Soviet Union. The American ruling class was never taken to task for its support of fascism, and escaped any serious consequences.

6

The Wake-up Call

My father died in 1987. I still have many of his books, reflecting his fascination with politics and the media. They include a wonderful treatise on the Cold War called *The Cold War and Its Origins* by D. F. Fleming, published by Doubleday in 1961. Fleming was a respected professor from Vanderbilt University. The book has long been out of print, but it is still a fascinating read. I often look at my father's copy, with its hundreds of markings and comments, and wonder what he would have thought of our world today.

The day my father died, each member of the family was allowed to give his or her last respects privately and spend time alone with dad. That day I promised him that I would carry the torch for him and do whatever I could do to help the truth be told about how our great country has been misled. It was a highly emotional experience for me. I believe to this day I am still mentored by his spirit.

At the time of my father's death, Anita and I had been successful consultants and CPAs. After twenty years, however, we did not have the wealth to make large donations to the organizations we wanted to support. Anita and I made the decision that if we ever had the means, we would give as much as we could to support political and charitable causes. We wanted to be more creative about our donations rather than just giving to old line charities. It's not that we didn't want to support the traditional organizations, but we were particularly interested in causes that were educational, scientific, and political.

Around the time my father died we changed directions in our business. We became venture capitalists just as that path was becoming lucrative. We founded our company, Paradigm Group, in 1991, and got involved in visionary, growth-oriented companies in industries like high tech and biotech.

We were fortunate to have reaped great financial rewards during the 1990s, and, true to our word, we were at last ready to participate in lots of philanthropic causes, and even to get involved with politics. I had also been able to influence my wife Anita's thinking over the years, with the insight my father had passed down. Like me, she was a passionate liberal. I knew that if Anita got involved in the political world, she would lead the charge more effectively than I to make a meaningful difference in the world.

Anita had been a concert pianist, and was considered a child prodigy. At the age of twelve she won a major music competition sponsored by the *Chicago Tribune,* and played with The Chicago Symphony Orchestra. As an adult, she changed paths completely and became an accountant. We knew each other as children and went to the same schools. When she switched to an accounting major, she became a student of mine in a CPA review course I was teaching. She was the first woman supervisor at the Illinois Department of Revenue and had forty auditors working under her supervision.

As we became more involved in politics from 1996 to 2000, Anita and I were fortunate to get the chance to meet some the most important and powerful people in the United States, including President Clinton, Hillary Clinton, and VicePresident Al Gore and his wife, Tipper. Although we met them through our political contributions to their candidacies, we found we had a number of common interests. Over time I felt they became friends, and that we were not just political and financial supporters. Like anyone who knew the Clintons personally, Anita and I agonized over the media's lurid handling of the Monica Lewinsky story, and over how shabbily the press treated the President Clinton and Vice President Gore, both of whom were devoted to serving their country. A lot of important news about the nation and the world was neglected in those years, while the owners of the press could make fortunes on what was essentially a tabloid story.

In fact, we noticed there were many things going on during the '90s that the press minimized or never reported, events that are coming out today—stories about terrorism, politics, and world events that should have been reported.

Given my view of the media handed down to me by my father, and my belief in its willingness to succumb to the direction of its corporate masters, I knew the scandals that swirled around the Clintons were fueled and kept alive by the media. I wanted to convey the lessons of the past to our political friends, but most of Washington was so enchanted and indoctrinated by media coverage and attention, that we could not convince people that the media was the problem. As the election of 2000 unfolded, all that would soon change.

By the way, it's not that I think there is a formal conspiracy. I just believe that endemic to the system today is a profound lack of intellectual independence. Even when you talk to distinguished reporters, many of them clearly think they are independent. But when I have asked them whether they have any control over what news is reported, they all admit that it's the editors that control the output. Reporters have little to say about what actually gets published; corporations are not democratic.

At one time editors possessed a mind of their own, and had the authority to make critical decisions, with the trust of the publisher behind them. But I believe, for the most part, the days of independent news organizations are long past. Today, too often the news is nothing more than a mixture of entertainment and corporate press releases designed to manipulate viewers and satisfy sponsors. News reporting is all about more profit and power for corporate interests and elites.

Even with my tough view of the media and its corporate masters, I was not prepared for what would happen in the days leading up to the next presidential election.

The election of 2000 left me in shock. I was far from alone; that election and its aftermath left over half the American voters in shock.

Though I had always suspected corruption and cronyism in some of our leaders and the media, the reality was far worse than I could ever have believed. Leading up to election, the media had trashed Vice President Al Gore unmercifully. They had failed to report many negative stories about Bush that were available during the campaign. Many of the stories about Bush later documented in *Fahrenheit 9/11* were known in 2000, but never discussed by the major media during the campaign.

Even before year 2000, Anita and I were aware of the story of George Bush Jr.'s days in the military, including the AWOL episode, as well as the Harken insider trading story, and the sale of the Texas Rangers by Bush to Tom Hicks for $250 million.

Bush was the managing general partner of the company that owned the Texas Rangers baseball team since 1989. While the governor of Texas, Bush allowed Hicks and his investment fund, Hicks, Muse, Tate & Furst Incorporated to manage $9 billion of the University of Texas endowment fund. As an investment manager myself, I am aware Hicks must have earned at least twice as much on managing the $9 billion as he did on the $250 million he paid for the baseball team. As governor and owner of the team, Bush effectively gave Hicks the money to buy the team that made Bush a multimillionaire. What a country.

In a similar case in 1971, Otto Kerner, the former Governor of Illinois, was convicted of income tax evasion and public corruption for signing legislation that helped increase the value of race track stock he owned. In Kerner's case he made about $150,000. In Bush's circumstance, he made $12 million on the Rangers' sale. I worked on the Kerner case when I was with the IRS from 1967 to 1971, and wrote an analysis of the Rangers case for reporters to review, and to give context to the Bush/Hicks "situation." Some might call it a bribe. But there was no follow up, as was the case with most stories of Bush's business history.

We observed how the media was focusing only on Gore's trivial misstatements of facts, sending the message that Gore was a liar or, at least loved to exaggerate. Shortly after the election we got information from many reporters that media giants like Jack Welch, GE chairman, and others were going to do anything they could to get Bush elected. Why?

Because I believe that just like Tom Hicks' deal in Texas, Bush promised them a *quid pro quo.* If Bush were elected he made it clear, with acts like his appointment of Michael Powell—Colin Powell's son—that Bush would continue the policy of media deregulation that was a windfall for the corporate media conglomerates.

This exchange of favors is as old as the hills. Though most people are aware of the classic image of the "bag man" delivering cash, in Washington, the more sophisticated form is the *quid pro quo;* do a favor for me and I'll do one for you.

After the 2000 election, Anita and I had several conversations with Al and Tipper Gore discussing how the media had recklessly destroyed Gore's campaign, turning the election into a popularity contest instead of a battle over issues. The Gores were fully aware of the media's influence on the results of the 2000 election, as well as the lack of reporting on what was really behind the recount fiasco in Florida. The Gores wanted do something about it, and they thought we could help.

They invited Anita and me to a conference in Memphis sponsored by Vice President Gore's Political Action Committee, called Leadership '02.

The conference took place in July of 2002. There were about one hundred of Gore's closest supporters in the group. The first day of the conference, there were several small break out sessions, with a group leader assigned to each one. At the end of the first session, the group leaders reported on these mini-meetings.

I was sitting with my wife, Anita, and Kerry Kennedy Cuomo after a breakout session and we were all in agreement that the real problem was how to get our message out in the current media climate.

Most of the others in the group were focusing on strategies for the next election. Finally, encouraged by my wife, I stood up and told the group that in my opinion the media was the real problem. There was no way to challenge the media now because of the major concentration of ownership in the hands of fewer and fewer corporations. That alone would prevent the media from being independent enough to represent the people, as opposed to the powerful elites who had a greater interest in these corporations and their well-being. No issues or strategies would work unless we addressed this issue.

With that, Debbie Stabenow, the U.S. Senator from Michigan, jumped up like a jack-in-the-box and passionately supported my position. She proceeded to discuss some of the same issues Anita and I had with the press. Senator Stabenow and the rest of the Democratic caucuses in both the House and Senate had personally experienced some of the damaging side effects to our democracy brought about by the power of the press. She told the group that she could not get meaningful media coverage when the Democratic caucus would call for a news conference about important legislation.

By the time the conference ended, everyone agreed action was in order. We needed to do something about the media's distortions and lack of true reporting on real issues. After the conference, we solicited the help of Vice President Gore and Senator Stabenow by sharing something I had written a few months earlier.

It was a memorandum which essentially outlined the idea that talk radio was the only media that could hope to address the issues we had raised, with the limited resources available. If we could develop a true working plan for some type of more responsible media outlet, and work together with people in politics to find financial supporters, we had a chance to change the status quo we all found so disheartening. It would take dedication but all of us believed it could be done. It had to be done.

They were more than willing to help. We had the rough outline of a plan to change the media. The seed to Air America had just been planted.

7

Getting Connected

In May of 2002, before Vice President Al Gore's Leadership 2002 conference, Anita and I had attended two prominent Progressive Donor conferences conducted by Mike Lux and Robert Borosage. Mike Lux is the head of the Progressive Donor Network, or PDN, and had worked for the Clinton White House. PDN focuses on progressive strategy, and includes many former political advisors and policy makers. He had all the political contacts you could want. Bob is the head of Take Back America, a non-profit progressive organization supported by many people from Hollywood and the entertainment industry. Take Back America's focus is on raising awareness around important progressive issues. Both had become good friends of ours, and we had previously sponsored several of their events. Mike and Bob eventually became members of AnShell's advisory board.

Mike and Bob knew everyone who was anyone in liberal and progressive circles. They were extremely helpful in giving us help contacting prominent and wealthy people for the radio network we were planning.

The list was a who's who of people who could help fund the project. At the PDN conference I sat next to Christie Hefner as we watched a series of prominent speakers, including James Carville and Paul Begala. Christie is CEO of *Playboy Magazine*, and herself a publisher, yet even she was also frustrated with the media for the same reasons we all were. She and her husband Bill Marovitz, a major political figure in Illinois, were sympathetic to our ideas, but warned me that there are too many barriers to getting into the media. The biggest was money. There was talk of Norman Lear and Barbra Streisand funding a liberal cable channel, but that would cost at least one billion dollars. I asked if any other plans were in the works because a cable station does not reach a very large audience. CNN at best reaches only two million people per week while Rush Limbaugh is reaching twenty million per week on over six hundred stations. It seemed logical to me that a liberal radio network would be far cheaper than cable and reach a much larger audience. That's when I began to work on the concept I would introduce at Vice President Al Gore's July Leadership 2002 event.

But I did more than just imagine. I did research, organized my thoughts, and put my ideas on paper. I then asked Bob Borosage for contact information for two of the most progressive personalities, Barbra Streisand and Norman Lear. In June 2002 I contacted Ms. Streisand through her manager and Mr. Lear directly, sending them a memo of my plan. Here it is: the blueprint for Air America Radio.

MEMORANDUM

```
From: Sheldon Drobny
Date: June 1, 2002
Re: Independent Broadcast News
```

```
I have done a preliminary study of the broadcast mar-
ket including radio and television including cable TV.
I have also reviewed the history of the success of
right wing talk radio and the evolution of its suc-
cess and domination of talk radio throughout the major
markets. In that analysis I also reviewed the televi-
sion market for news and talk shows, especially cable
```

TV, to get a further understanding of that market in order to develop an efficient and cost effective strategy to enter this market.

The first conclusion that became obvious is that there is no way to effectively enter the TV talk and news market. The cost would be prohibitive and the three major cable news channels, CNN, Fox, and MSNBC dominate that market. Fox has won the war of the right wing and has captured that market while CNN has drifted somewhat left and right and has managed to infuriate both sides. MSNBC was successful for a while in appealing to the right wing while Clinton was the President, but its ratings have suffered since and accordingly they are moving to the left a bit as noted by their hiring Phil Donahue. MSNBC has identified an audience of progressives to try to increase their ratings.

The one interesting anomaly I observed was that the most successful right wing talk radio hosts do not necessarily do well on news and talk TV. As a matter of fact, it is radio where one can get away with the most absurd, radical, and intellectually dishonest programming. The power of visual media exposes the appearance and body language and the dishonesty of these people. As dissatisfied as I am with television news, at least the visual aspects are somewhat self correcting to expose the real demagogues.

Given the preceding analysis, it is clear that news and talk radio is the best approach to getting out a more independent and progressive message. In doing that, it would be advisable to use the same approach as that used by Rush Limbaugh when he started his radio show in Sacramento and gained popularity, leading ultimately to syndication and the copycats that now dominate right wing talk radio. In addition, as previously mentioned, radio allows more leeway for progressive talk hosts to get angry and "rattle peoples' cages." There are already some very good progressive talk show hosts, but their success has been limited because they are usually blended into the same stations that present right wing hosts at prime times. It is very difficult to get a progressive message out in talk radio when the stations controlling this sector are presenting progressive shows on weekends and evening hours. Just as CNN and MSNBC are suffering from a somewhat schizophrenic approach about their message, a talk radio station generally must make a decision as to which viewpoint they will profile; the left or the right. To my knowledge, there are no news or talk radio stations that have a progressive leaning or profile progressive hosts.

Now is the time to strike. There are several radio stations that are not talk or news oriented that are either having ratings problems or are considering changing their format. It appears that the only alternative today for progressives to listen to independent news is to listen to NPR. However, NPR has its limitations in that its programming is not exclusively news and has much content that is not particularly appealing to a mass audience. They also have limitations as to their content because they are a charitable organization. NPR is far more independent than the other stations, but it cannot get the progressive message out to the mainstream public. Progressives can appeal just as well to main stream Americans, but the message must be simpler and more direct.

Ninety percent of the country is not sophisticated about the political world, so they tend to listen to the simplest message that satisfies their personal frustrations. In the movie *Network News,* the crazy news show host initiated the slogan: "I'm mad as hell and am not going to take it anymore." We are on the right side of the issues, but our arguments are too complex and seem to be vague in terms of immediate personal benefit to the average listener. That message can be given by getting to new stations that are changing their direction and presenting a plan for them that will appeal to their corporate owners. Corporations do not intrinsically have a political philosophy. As a matter of fact, their only interest is making more money. As Hubble said in the movie *The*

Way We Were, "...when it is convenient for a Fascist producer to make a movie with a Communist director, they'll do it..." The bottom line is all that counts in corporate America. It is our job to convince them that it is in their interest.

CONCLUSION

It is my opinion that the best way to penetrate the talk radio market is through existing radio stations that will change to talk and news radio. These stations must profile progressive talk show hosts, and also should present the other side with weekend and late evening right wing alternatives just for balance. We work with the experts in syndication and get some good candidates for entertaining high profile progressive hosts. We can even buy a radio station in a smaller market for a reasonable price to test market the concept. Even if the concept fails, the station will still have good residual value and can be sold without a significant loss. I believe that this is the most cost effective approach to the project that minimizes our capital outlay which in any event would be fully tax deductible in contrast to non-deductible donations to political causes. I believe that with this sensible approach, we can in the long run change the attitudes of the main stream listening public.

I even referred to the movie, *The Way We Were.* I thought it would get Barbra's attention. I got negative responses from both parties.

But we now had a concrete outline of our concept for a progressive liberal talk radio syndication company. After Gore's Leadership Conference, we had some political support. We decided to present the plan to America's progressive liberals and see if we could raise funds. It was starting to look like we could actually turn our idea into a reality.

It was time to make it official—we were ready to put a company together and write a business plan.

8

Lost History

Even as Anita and I moved forward towards our vision, my thoughts returned to the past, back to the lessons of my father, Charles Drobny.

As we thought about forming a new media company, it was impossible to forget what had happened to liberals in the past. Over the years—again through reading, research, and the experiences passed on to me by my father—I had formed an opinion of the collaboration between industry and the press, and what happens to the people who try to resist it. I thought back to the story of Henry Wallace, Franklin Delano Roosevelt's Vice President.

I've already said that the American firms who profited by arms sales to Germany were worried that their activities would be exposed after the war. This Wall Street crowd hated FDR from the start. Their hatred was so vicious that they actually accused FDR of being a Bolshevik. Roosevelt did not like them any better than they liked him.

Roosevelt was very much concerned about the appeasement of Hitler during the 1930s; he was one of the few world leaders who wanted to stop Hitler before he became too powerful. But FDR had many domestic problems caused by the Depression, and, furthermore, the American public was isolationist in its attitude towards the rest of the world. He was unable to act on his concern.

Many U.S. newspapers, early on, had praised Hitler for his success in rebuilding Germany in the 1930s and kept a comfortable distance from activities in Hitler's Nazi Germany. But that obviously changed as the war unfolded and Hitler's atrocities were revealed. By the time Americans entered the war, the American supporters of the Nazi war machine knew there would be postwar consequences of the public knowing of their activities, once Hitler was defeated. The November 1944 election was instrumental in preventing that scandal from ever seeing the light of day.

The 1944 Democratic Convention was held in July that year, in Chicago. There was no doubt that FDR would be re-nominated. Vice President Wallace was also expected to be re-nominated as his running mate. Wallace was a progressive and a supporter of labor and civil rights. In addition, like Roosevelt, he was a strong supporter of a postwar friendship with the USSR. Wallace believed that the only reasonable strategy at that point in time was to come to a peaceful postwar agreement with the USSR. Russia had lost nearly twenty-five million people including ten million civilians, and their country needed to be rebuilt. A friendship with such a devastated nation seemed like the best possible scenario for all parties.

Henry Wallace was firmly grounded in the liberal tradition. Although a single word cannot define or characterize a political philosophy, the word "liberal" in America today generally refers to one who is receptive to change and new ideas in social terms, and approves of the positive role of government in our lives. Liberalism has its roots in nineteenth century Europe, when freedom from the dominance of church, aristocracy and absolute state authority became an ascending value. Liberals tend to be concerned with social justice, individual civil liberties, freedom of the press, and the common good; and they expect government to uphold these values.

Wallace was a liberal in the tradition of FDR because he supported an unproven yet reasonable idea that good relations with the post war Soviet Union was a good idea, something that conservatives abhorred. The Soviet system was perceived as a threat to capitalism in the minds of the conservatives. However, the reality was that the Russians had sacrificed dearly during the war and were entitled to a chance of a cooperative relationship.

America was at a critical juncture at the end of the war, in terms of its relation to the Soviet Union. According to Alderman Edwin M. Burke, co-author of a 1996 book with R. Craig Sautter and Richard M. Daley called *Inside the Wigwam,* the 1944 Chicago Democratic Convention was the stage on which the very political future of America itself was played.

Burke's book is a history of Chicago Presidential Conventions from 1860-1996. At the Democratic convention of 1944, the party bosses around the country knew FDR was seriously ill and was not likely to finish his fourth term. The idea of Wallace being the next President was a terrifying thought to those in the conservative and southern wing of the Democratic Party. They were strongly anti-Soviet and knew Wallace was disposed towards normalizing relations with the USSR.

Unlike Roosevelt, who was a shrewd politician, Wallace was a true idealist. Although Roosevelt was very progressive in his policies, he knew that the coalition of southern and conservative Democrats was necessary for the Democrats to win a national election. The party bosses in Chicago, including Chicago Mayor Ed Kelly, intervened just as Wallace was about to be re-nominated. Kelly instructed the Chicago Fire Commissioner at the time to close down the convention hall. The party bosses wanted Harry Truman to be nominated because Truman was part of Missouri machine politics and could easily be manipulated in the postwar policy toward the Soviet Union.

The party bosses succeeded in getting Truman to be FDR's running mate in a dramatic and brilliant series of political maneuvers.

As Wallace was being nominated, Mayor Kelly had the fire commissioner evacuate the Chicago Stadium. He did it by engineering and artificially creating a fire hazard. The Chicago Stadium doors were opened to the skid row bums in the neighborhood. People poured into the convention in droves, causing the overcrowding of the building, which then had to be evacuated because of fire hazard limits. That nomination was postponed for a day. Party bosses quickly took over the process by "arm twisting" the delegates to switch their allegiance to Truman. The next day, Mayor Kelly had ushers—hired by the city—screen people as they entered the hall. They picked out the Wallace supporters and prevented many of them from being admitted.

The nomination of Harry Truman as Vice President and the death of FDR in April, 1945 made it much less likely that Wall Street would be exposed to a the scandal that would have exposed their support of Hitler. It's not that the machine politicians at the Democratic Convention had any particular sympathy for the Wall Street collaborators with Nazi Germany, or lacked ideals. But many of these Democrats were pragmatists. From their business dealings, they knew that Wallace was perceived by the business establishment as even worse than Roosevelt. The Wall Street industrialists also wanted him out as well—which is not to say conservative Democrats conspired with the Wall Street Nazi collaborators. Their interests, however, happened to align, and created a common intention to undermine Wallace's re-nomination. Machine politicians do not want honest idealists as party heads, and their corrupt practices would not be tolerated by a man like Wallace.

It also set in motion events that would dramatically change the postwar relations between the Soviet Union and the Military Industrial Complex. Unlike Roosevelt, Truman was not able to control the conservative Democrats who were composed mainly of Southern segregationists and right wing militarists. FDR had known the danger of this group, but as a master politician, he also knew he needed them to get elected. Roosevelt recognized Stalin was a ruthless dictator domestically, but again, he had needed his cooperation during the war, and so treated "Uncle Joe" like any other corrupt-but-necessary political boss. In other words, Roosevelt was a pragmatist; he knew that without the cooperation of Stalin, there could not be a lasting peace in the postwar period.

But Roosevelt's peace with the USSR was never to be. He died in April, 1945. The postwar Truman doctrine of confrontation with the Soviet Union became the linchpin of American postwar policy. This eventually led to the ascendance of the Military Industrial Complex that Eisenhower would warn us about so clearly.

Truman's policy of containment satisfied the Wall Street industrialists for three reasons. First, by making Russia the enemy, these industrialists were able to demonize the Socialist Worker's Movement which at one time had been a powerful force for change in the United States. Second, it allowed the arms industry to continue the business they had so effectively begun with Nazi Germany. Finally, they were able to distract attention from their activities in which they were beneficiaries of the American Government's covert use of former Nazis in the Cold War fight. If the American government was making secret use of once-powerful Nazi officers, these individuals' deeds would never be exposed to the public—nor would the deeds of their collaborators.

One can never know what would have happened had FDR lived, or if Henry Wallace had eventually gone on to replace him. One only knows that today the symbiotic relationship between the military and the armament industrialists has grown out of control. The growth of the defense industry has sapped U.S. resources, increased the "demand" for war, and put an increasingly larger concentration of wealth and power in the hands of a few.

Back at the 1944 Democratic Convention in Chicago the coup by the "right wing of the Democratic Party" that put Truman in charge was never reported in the popular media. It is not part of

American history. Ostensibly, according to the press, Wallace was simply not nominated because he was considered too controversial. The newspapers reported only that the Chicago Stadium was closed because of a mysterious fire hazard. But in reality, Wallace had actually been popular with the delegates, and only "controversial" after the fact. When the convention reconvened it took not one, but two ballots to get Truman nominated.

This suppression of liberal values and ideas is nothing short of a danger to democracy. That's what true believers in democracy are fighting against—the forces that are will go to any length to stop the will of the people from being enacted. With our vision of a progressive radio network, we wanted to make it more difficult for deceit, manipulation and back room pressure to win the day. Anita and I believe that in politics, as in nature, balance is necessary among forces. Dialogue between conservatives and liberals is what informs the democratic process, and produces the enactment of reasonable legislation and governance. The domination of either side is not in the best interests of the United States, let alone the world.

Our vision for Air America Radio was not liberal domination. It was a place where liberals could contribute to the debate and discourse between opposing and sincere points of view, in a time when that debate is almost entirely dominated by the conservative media. We believe balance must be restored. Otherwise government cannot serve the best interests of the people. In politics, it is the stability caused by opposite and equal forces that makes for sustainable and enduring systems.

9

In Business

The company we formed was called AnShell Media, LLC. The company's name is a combination of the names Anita and Shelly. It's a common, even old-fashioned way of naming a family-owned business. We got the idea from the movie company called Miramax, started by Harvey Weinstein and his brother Bob, who named their company for their parents, Miriam and Max.

We now had an official entity to represent us, and armed with a great concept and people willing to help us contact rich and powerful liberals, we began to write an official business plan. For this we turned to the business Anita and I had started, called Paradigm Group.

We used Paradigm Group, a venture capital company, to provide the seed capital for AnShell. AnShell, in turn, became one of our portfolio companies. This is a standard way of funding a good idea in the venture capital world. Using the company's venture capital fund, we raised two million dollars that would pay for salaries of staff, organizing expenses, travel, and more.

Paradigm Group, as an investment firm, has written and reviewed thousands of business plans. The company immediately set about writing a crackerjack business plan for AnShell Media. For this, we turned to one of the newer members of the Paradigm Group: Javier Saade.

Saade had joined the firm in September of 2002. He became a managing director and investment analyst for us after working for a prominent financial consulting firm. We told him we wanted him to do the research and write a business plan for a liberal talk radio syndication company. As with any start-up business, we needed to get an objective review of that business sector, and of the efficacy of the opportunity.

Not only was Javier a great choice because he was a Harvard MBA with experience in business consulting; he was also objective about the plan. Javier was agnostic about politics. He not only helped write the plan, but he became so convinced of its success that he later went to work for Air America.

The first business plan AnShell came up with was a modest approach to launching a syndicated program of liberal talk radio. In our research we had learned that Rush Limbaugh actually started his show locally in Sacramento on an obscure AM radio station. He had been a Top 40 disc jockey for a number of years before he started his talk show.

At the time, AM radio was dying. The AM signal was not adaptable to music and that's where the radio business was going. Over the years, FM bands had become the most valuable in radio because they are so superior for broadcasting music. Many AM station owners were ready to give up, when Limbaugh appeared. Rush Limbaugh actually saved AM radio with his experiment in talk radio.

Talk radio suited the AM frequencies because talk doesn't require great sound quality. Rush's show was a success locally, and grew in popularity until it was syndicated throughout the country in the '80s. The Clinton era only increased his popularity, and he became the most successful and highly paid talk show host in history.

We also learned that there was indeed opportunity; reviewing the 45 top rated talk show stations in America, we learned that there was 310 hours of conservative talk broadcast each week. In comparison, these stations broadcasted only 5 hours of talk that could be called progressive or liberal.

Keeping in mind Limbaugh's success as a radio personality, we thought our business plan should include one seasoned liberal talk show host who had demonstrated an organic growth pattern similar to Rush's. We wanted to put our foot in the water. Our choice for this lead host was Mike Malloy.

I had heard Mike when he was the only liberal voice on WLS in Chicago, an ABC affiliate that broadcast Rush and other Rush clones during the day. Later, in 2002, Mike was broadcasting on IE America Radio, which was an innovative attempt to use streaming internet to broadcast a full day of liberal radio.

IE America Radio was formed and owned by the United Auto Workers Union. The UAW lost over $20 million in this venture because they overestimated the power of the internet and never got affiliate radio stations to pick up their content. Before Mike went to IE, he had a terrific show on WLS in Chicago. He broadcast from Chicago from 10 P.M. to 1 A.M. weekdays and did very well in that time slot. But he also got lots of complaints from the mostly right wing audience of that station, and just couldn't last in that environment. You can't just drop a progressive show in the middle of a day of full blown conservatism and expect it to work.

The idea of formatic purity was something that my memo had addressed to Barbra Streisand and Norman Lear. IE America Radio, for example, had been an all liberal station, so listeners knew they could tune into a station with consistent content. This has been the general approach in radio since the dominance of television in the early '50s. Radio had become a niche market appealing primarily to the tastes of the listener. The problem with IE was that the expectations of internet radio were far greater than reality. However, the idea was good and made a lot of sense.

We contacted Mike in the late summer of 2002, thinking he might be interested in our concept. Not only did he want to be involved, Mike did something that, perhaps more than anything else, would help make Air America a reality. In an attempt to help us he introduced Anita and me to the person he described as the smartest talk radio guy in the business, Jon Sinton.

Jon was a seasoned radio consultant and entrepreneur. Both Malloy and Sinton lived in Atlanta. He had been the executive producer of a Jim Hightower's show, a syndicated program that made a stab at a liberal response to people like Rush Limbaugh. Hightower is an impassioned agitator and former agriculture commissioner of Texas who has been trying to wake up the population for years.

The first thing Jon Sinton said when he heard our concept for a syndicated liberal radio programming was "please go away and lose my phone number." Perhaps it was because of the Hightower experience; he thought a syndicated program at this point was a waste of time. Based on his experience, putting a liberal program into what was most likely to be a conservative talk radio environment made about as much sense as putting "Led Zeppelin on a classical station" as Jon says.

The only road Jon was interested in going down with AnShell was the one that led to an all liberal, twenty-four-day broadcast. A real radio network.

This was very different from what we had planned. It meant changing AnShell's direction from a syndication company that started with a single talk show, to a full-fledged 24/7 network. It would require a lot more than the $10 million we expected our original plan to cost, and in fact would take world class fundraising. It would be very tough. After some consideration, and discussion with Anita, we agreed to try. But Jon Sinton was hesitating; he wasn't sure we could make it happen.

10

Planning the Road Show

By November 2002 our preliminary business plan was complete, with potential management and initial talent in place. We were ready to go on the road to start raising money from potentially wealthy supporters. In the investment world, this is known as "the road show." It is a common event, where a Power Point or other audiovisual presentation is used to reach an audience of prospective investors. It's usually done by investment banking firms when they are trying to raise capital for a private company, or get indications of interest for an initial public offering.

Paradigm had raised hundreds of millions of dollars on such road shows from our usual investors. However, in the past, the investors would only evaluate a deal based upon its business merits. We thought it would be much easier to raise money for AnShell than any of our previous investments because of its political implications.

Not only did we have a great business plan, but thanks to Mike Lux of the Progressive Doner Network and other contacts, we had a list of passionate supporters of the liberal cause who also were among the richest and most powerful people in the country.

Our first meeting took place in November 2002 in California at the home of Arianna Huffington. We had contacted her because she was a recent convert to the liberal cause and was leading the charge to change the political landscape. She invited us to a fundraiser she was hosting for Salon.com, a sophisticated internet-based magazine.

Arianna Huffington is an influential and well-respected columnist. Anita and I took Javier Saade and Jon Sinton with us. The event at Arianna's was actually a road show for Salon. In the late '90s Salon raised over $20 million in an initial public offering or IPO. At that time it was easy to raise money for any dot.com company, and Salon was no exception, even though it is a content-oriented site as opposed to service-oriented site. However, with the dot.com bust in 2000, Salon needed more money, and Arianna had agreed to host the event for David Talbot, Salon's CEO. Bill Hambrecht, a prominent investment banker and passionate liberal, was underwriting the new round of investments for Salon. We thought this would be a great opportunity to meet wealthy Hollywood folks even though the fundraiser was for Salon.

There were several well known people at that meeting, including Norman and Lynn Lear, Ed Asner and his wife Cindy, Tracey Ullman, and Morgan Fairchild, among others. This was the first time that Anita and I had attended one of these Hollywood gatherings, and we really enjoyed it. Without even mentioning AnShell, we were a hit at that meeting because we supported the idea that Salon was an important independent publication and should be funded by the people in the room. I even had the chance, in a Q&A session, to talk to the group about my favorite subject: the corporate-owned media. Many people at that meeting asked for our business cards and gave us theirs. People were clearly passionate about their politics, and hungry for a voice in the media that could be heard supporting their point of view. At that meeting, Jon Sinton said to me that he was on board. AnShell Media now had a full time CEO.

When we arrived home after the meeting, we were convinced that if Salon appealed to the Hollywood group, AnShell Media would have even more appeal; after all, our company would be a full blown attack against Rush Limbaugh, Sean Hannity, Bill O' Reilly, and their ilk on radio, with a much wider audience than Salon had.

We began to fine-tune our concept, deciding to take it to the highly political Washington, D.C. crowd for real scrutiny. With his connections in the Beltway, Mike Lux could help. He scheduled a meeting in December, 2002 with John Podesta in DC.

John Podesta had been Chief of Staff for Bill Clinton during his second term. Our friend Mike Lux had told us Podesta was planning to form a think tank to counteract the many conservative think tanks in Washington. That think tank would eventually become the Center for American Progress, whose mission, to quote Podesta, is "to find progressive and pragmatic solutions to significant domestic and international problems."

Lux was a former Clinton aide and good friend of Podesta. We thought a liberal talk radio network might be a perfect outlet for someone like Podesta, and hoped we could get his support and advice.

The meeting with John Podesta included Mike Lux and former Clinton press secretary Joe Lockhart. We met for breakfast meeting at a downtown DC hotel. In the meeting we learned that Podesta, Lux, and Lockhart had put together a three-pronged plan, which included a for-profit media company to attack the conservatives. The think tank was one of the other legs and they had also conceived of political action group as the third leg. We advanced the cause for AnShell to be part of their so-called three legged stool.

Podesta had to leave the breakfast meeting before the others because he had another meeting, but Joe Lockhart stayed a while longer. We asked him what he thought about John's reaction to our company. Podesta does not show his emotions in a meeting. It was hard for Anita and me to get a read on him. Joe Lockhart, to our surprise, told us that Podesta loved our idea and would be very supportive of our plan. We were very pleased and thanked Joe for his analysis of the meeting. We now seemed to have the support of some key figures in California and Washington.

The next week in December 2002 I received a call from the *New York Times* media reporter, Jim Rutenberg. He had heard about AnShell and wanted to do a story about us. The word was already out.

11

Launch Number One

Although I've made my feelings about the major media clear, that feeling only applies to management—not necessarily to reporters. I knew Jim Rutenberg was a good reporter. Evidently he had received some information about AnShell from one of his sources.

I had learned from past experiences with the press that one has to be very careful about going on the record. I had a good relationship with reporters in Chicago that had covered me, as well as the Paradigm Group when it was newsworthy. I also learned that if a reporter has a story about you from one of his sources, it is usually better to help the reporter with your own version of the story so you can control the agenda. This is not the conventional wisdom, but I have never been one who follows conventional wisdom. In my opinion, the only time not to talk to the press is when there is a criminal investigation about you. Otherwise, the press could give you a terrific opportunity to promote your point or cause.

That is exactly what I was thinking when Rutenberg called me one December day. He proceeded to tell me he was going to run a New Year's holiday story in *The New York Times* about liberal media projects throughout America. I asked him what information he had about AnShell, and what he told me was pretty accurate. I asked him why he was interested in a fledgling company like ours since in my experience, a company at AnShell's stage of development was not newsworthy. Rutenberg told me there was so little being done on the liberal side of media, that any company making even the smallest effort was worth reporting. I then planted the seed that would get AnShell millions of dollars worth of free publicity. I told Jim AnShell was not ready for prime time and that if he held off mentioning us in his holiday story, I would give him an exclusive about AnShell. We didn't want to be mixed into the small and fragmented not-for-profit organizations that were doing small projects to counteract the major media. He kept his part of the bargain and so did I.

To be treated seriously, we had to be both a business and a media story. I called Jon Sinton, and we immediately started working on getting the organization ramped up and ready for a good *New York Times* story.

By this time—December 2002—Vice President Al and Tipper Gore also knew about AnShell, and had already talked with us and given us advice. I told Al about the *New York Times* reporter, hoping to solicit his help in getting some meat into the story. They were just completing a book tour for *Joined at the Heart* and said that their schedules would be much lighter after the first of the year. Anita and I planned a DC trip to meet Al and Tipper to strategize. I also had a concept I wanted to run by Gore; I wanted to propose to him that he join us as an editorial commentator, with a five-day-a-week, three minute short form show—much like Paul Harvey's.

For decades Paul Harvey has provided his own unique and recognizable syndicated commentaries. It is what is called in the radio business "short form" programming. We had learned in our research that Paul Harvey was earning millions and millions from that syndicated show. We thought former Vice President Al Gore would be the perfect person to do the same kind of pointed commentary.

We knew that if ABC was paying Paul Harvey a fortune, the show had to be very profitable. The other advantage of a short daily commentary from Al Gore, the man the people actually elected president in 2000, was that it would be much easier to slot into daily radio programming. Program directors would not have to change any of their current content to fit in a daily short commentary.

Al was already working on his own cable TV project and unfortunately could not get actively involved with AnShell at that time. He did promise to help the cause any way he could, and said he would revisit the short form show at an appropriate future date. Gore was true to his word, however, and help came almost immediately, in the form of an introduction to Al Franken.

Once we made a commitment to a 24/7 network format for our liberal radio concept, we knew we would need a nationally recognized talent as the centerpiece. While I was a huge fan of Mike Malloy, he did not provide the name recognition we needed.

There are few entertainers today who can mix form and content—comedy and politics—as skillfully as Al Franken. Gore had called Franken after our meeting because I had mentioned that he would be my dream host for the launch of AnShell. Unlike failed shows like Mario Cuomo and Jim Hightower's attempts at radio, Franken was an Emmy award winning writer and comedian who had worked for *Saturday Night Live* for many years. He could add the entertainment factor that was missing in liberal talk radio. I immediately got on the phone to talk to Franken.

In January of 2003, Al Franken was at Harvard University on a fellowship. Working together with students, Franken's fellowship would result in his bestseller, *Lies and the Lying Liars Who Tell Them: A Fair and Balanced Look at the Right,* published by Penguin/Dutton Books. For those who haven't read it, it is a meticulously reported exposé of the conservative media and its deceptive tactics.

When I talked to Franken he was reluctant to get involved because he was busy writing his book—plus he knew nothing about talk radio. Franken, like many others, was not convinced that liberal talk radio could succeed. I told him that I would give him data and research we had collected in our effort to build a liberal radio syndication company. The facts could speak for themselves. I explained that I was a venture capitalist, and I had good reason to believe that there was an untapped market out there. I was not interested in a failed venture just for the sake of a good cause. I suspected he would probably take this more seriously if I discussed the business aspects with him. He reserved his decision and waited to hear from our CEO Jon Sinton.

Jon Sinton and Javier Saade visited Franken on several occasions in late January and February of 2003 to try to convince him to come on board. In an attempt to show Al the huge potential of radio, I sent him an article written by an author named Thom Hartmann called "Talking Back To Talk Radio," which Thom had written for a liberal publication called *Common Dreams*.

Thom is a highly respected author who had spent the early part of his career in radio as a disc jockey. Thom and I could not have been more in tune with each other. After we discovered his article in December of 2002, we immediately contacted him to see if he could help us with AnShell. Not only was Thom a brilliant thinker, but in my opinion, he also had experience as a DJ in the '70s and understood the radio business. He agreed to help us in any way he could.

By forwarding Thom's article to Franken, we took a step towards convincing him there was a great business opportunity out there for any visionary in radio programming. Here is some of what Hartman said in his article:

> "The station programmers I've talked with who've tried a progressive or centrist talker for an hour or two, only to get angry responses from dittoheads, think this means only extreme-right-wing talkers (and, ideally, convicted felons or those who "declare war on liberals") will make money for their station. And, because they've already carved out the hard-right-Republican-talk niche and alienated the progressive/Democrat niche, they're right.

But for stations who want to get into talk in a market already dominated by right-wing talkers on competing stations, the irrefutable evidence of national elections and polls shows that believing only right-wingers will bring listeners (and advertisers) is a mistake. All they need do is what anybody with music programming experience would recommend: identify their niche and stick with it. (Cynics say stations won't program Democrats because owners and management are all "rich Republicans." To this I say they should listen to some of the music being profitably produced and programmed by America's largest publishing and broadcasting corporations. Profits, for better or worse, are relatively opinion-free.)

By running Democratic/progressive-talk in a programming day free of right-wing talkers, stations will open up a new niche and ride it to success. This is a particularly huge opportunity for music stations who look with envy at the success of talk stations in their market, but haven't been willing to jump in because all the best right-wing talkers are already on the competition: all they need do is put on progressive talkers, and they'll open a new, unserved, and profitable niche.

And, with right-wing ideologues now in charge of our government, the time has never been better: as Rush showed during the Clinton years (the peak of his success), "issues" talk thrives best in an underdog environment. It's in the American psyche to give a fair listen to people challenging the party in power."

Franken was convinced enough by this article to go on record as being in negotiations as AnShell's first line of talent. We were ready to go forward with *The New York Times* profile and all that that would bring.

12

On Our Way

From *The New York Times,* February 17, 2003:

Liberal Radio Is Planned by Rich Group of Democrats

by Jim Rutenberg

A group of wealthy Democratic donors is planning to start a liberal radio network to counterbalance the conservative tenor of radio programs like "The Rush Limbaugh Show."

The group, led by Sheldon and Anita Drobny, venture capitalists from Chicago who have been major campaign donors for Bill Clinton and Al Gore, is in talks with Al Franken, the comedian and author of *Rush Limbaugh Is a Big Fat Idiot.* It hopes to enlist other well-known entertainers with a liberal point of view for a 14-hour, daily slate of commercial programs that would heavily rely on comedy and political satire.

The plan faces several business and content challenges, from finding a network of radio stations to buy the program to overcoming the poor track record of liberal radio shows. But it is the most ambitious undertaking yet to come from liberal Democrats who believe they are overshadowed in the political propaganda wars by conservative radio and television personalities.

The concern has been around for years: Hillary Rodham Clinton first mentioned a "vast, right-wing conspiracy" in 1998. But the sentiment has taken on new urgency with the rise to the top of the cable news ratings of the Fox News Channel, considered by many to have a conservative slant, and the Republicans' gaining control of the Senate in November. Such events have spurred many wealthy Democrats to explore investments in possible, liberal-skewing media ventures. New campaign finance rules that restrict giving opportunities also gave them further incentive.

The new liberal radio network is initially being financed by the Paradigm Group, of which the Drobnys are the principal partners. Ms. Drobny is the chairwoman of the venture, which is being called AnShell Media L.L.C. Jon Sinton, a longtime, Atlanta-based radio executive, will be its chief executive. He helped start the nationally syndicated radio program of Jim Hightower, the former Texas agriculture commissioner. Liberals had hoped that would be their answer to Mr. Limbaugh, but it was canceled shortly after its start in the mid-1990s.

The failure of Mr. Hightower's show supported the notion of many in radio that liberal hosts do not have what it takes to become successful and entertaining hosts: the fire-and-brim-stone manner and a ready-made audience alienated by the mainstream news media it perceives to be full of liberal bias.

Mr. Sinton said the new venture would seek to disprove not only those who doubt liberal hosts can make it in radio, but also those who believe that success in radio depends on an alliance with one of the handful of major distributors or station groups.

The group said it was prepared to go it alone, selling its programming to the individual radio stations rather than go through a middleman. It has an initial investment of $10 million, which radio analysts said was enough to start up. Ms. Drobny said the cash would be placed in a fund that she hopes to grow to at least $200 million within the next year, which she hopes to use to finance other media ventures like the acquisition of radio stations and television production.

"The object of the programming is to be progressive and make a statement that counters this din from the right," Mr. Sinton said. "But we have a solid business plan that shows a hole in the market."

Many conservatives who assert the news media in general is infused with liberal bias say the premise of a liberal radio network is silly to begin with. But liberal Democrats say even if a liberal bias does exist, the mainstream news media strives for balance and fair play. They say their concern is that there are far fewer successful, outright partisan voices on the left than there are on the right.

"I feel like there's a monologue out there," Ms. Drobny said. "I just had this tremendous feeling with great passion that we had to make sure we're heard and make sure we're having a dialogue in this country of ours."

The list of successful conservative radio hosts is, in fact, fairly long Rush Limbaugh; Sean Hannity; Michael Savage; Michael Reagan. And there is no equivalent list of liberals. Past attempts, such as the programs of Mr. Hightower and Mario Cuomo, have failed.

Some radio executives said they simply did not believe liberal radio could become good business. Among them was Kraig T. Kitchen, chief executive of Premiere Radio Networks, one of the nation's largest radio syndication arms with the programs of Mr. Limbaugh, Mr. Reagan and Dr. Laura Schlessinger, among others. Though Mr. Kitchin said he was a conservative, he also said he would have pursued liberal programs had he thought there was money in them. He ascribes to the popular view in the industry that liberal hosts present issues in too much complexity to be very entertaining—while addressing a diffuse audience that has varying views.

"Individuals who are liberal in their viewpoints can be all-encompassing," he said. "It's very hard to define liberalism, unlike how easy it is to define conservatism. So, as a result, it doesn't evoke the same kind of passion as conservative ideologies do."

Mr. Sinton said he thought past attempts failed because they were not properly executed. He said he believed a big problem for Mr. Hightower was that his program was sandwiched into a schedule crammed with conservatives. "It is very hard to succeed when you throw liberal programming between bookends of Rush Limbaugh and Sean Hannity," he said. "That violates expectations of the listener."

This is why he said he was proposing a full slate of liberally skewing programming with morning, afternoon and early evening shows featuring hosts with as many big names in entertainment as possible.

"This side has failed by going at Rush, and trying to be Rush—you're not going to beat him at his game," Mr. Sinton said. "What really makes this work is tapping into Hollywood and New York and having a huge entertainment component, where political sarcasm is every bit as effective as Rush Limbaugh is at bashing you over the head."

Mr. Sinton acknowledged that his biggest challenge was in getting national distribution for the network. He said he would seek to strike deals with underperforming radio stations in major markets.

Analysts said that while the plan might seem difficult to achieve, it is not impossible. "It is going to be trickier in the top-10 markets, easier in the middle markets, but it will be possible," said Jonathan Jacoby, a radio industry analyst for SunTrust Robinson Humphrey. "There is a case that if they have the right product, they will be able to find distribution."

Talent, of course, will be key, Mr. Sinton acknowledged. A deal with Mr. Franken, the comedian, would help greatly in luring other big names, as well as in gaining distribution. He said he envisioned a daily program featuring Mr. Franken perhaps in the early afternoons (around the same time as "The Rush Limbaugh Show").

A representative for Mr. Franken, Henry Reisch of the William Morris Agency, said Mr. Franken was seriously considering the offer, and was mostly focusing on whether he could handle the commitment of a daily radio program. Judging from his comments as a guest last month on Phil Donahue's program on MSNBC, Mr. Franken would probably take a far different approach from that of Mr. Limbaugh. "I think the audience isn't there for a liberal Rush," he said. "Because I think liberals don't want to hear that kind of demagoguery."

© New York Times

We had hoped to make a splash with the exposure of a *New York Times* article. We definitely succeeded. On February 17, 2003, our web site was overwhelmed by emails from passionate liberals, radio station owners, talk show hosts and people who wanted to help in any way they could. There were so many emails we couldn't answer them all. It looked like there really was a hungry liberal audience out there. Now the challenge was delivering what so many were desperate for, judging from our emails: another kind of voice in the political discourse.

On the day the article appeared, Jon Sinton and I were contacted by every producer of every major news network. They all wanted interviews. The most persistent producers were from Fox News Channel. This is what we thought would happen. We suspected these right wing stations saw us as potential competition, though our audience is completely different. I suspected they wanted to use their interviews with us in order to trash us.

I refused to do any interviews with any of the major networks but I agreed to do an interview for the NPR show, *Talk of the Nation.* I thought NPR would be reasonably objective about an interview with us—compared to places like Fox.

Sinton became the face of AnShell Media for the other network interviews. The publicity snowballed. Thanks to the *Times* article, we now had the attention of a much larger population. And not just any population—with such wide exposure, we had gotten the attention of wealthy liberals who had contributed hundreds of millions of dollars to progressive candidates. Surely these people would rally to our cause, bringing their contributions with them. From our perspective—looking back it may seem naïve—we believed all we had to do was build our liberal radio network and the money would come. With the Iraq war on the horizon, surely reasonable rich liberals would see the urgency of our getting on the air before the next presidential election a year and a half away.

13

The Psychology
of Money

Although I know the difficulty any new company has raising money, Anita and I really thought this project would be different. We sincerely believed wealthy progressives would write checks as readily as leaves fall in autumn. After all, they had donated hundreds of millions of dollars to sleep in the Lincoln Bedroom and attend cocktail parties with the Clintons, Gores, and other major politicians. Barbra Streisand sang at President Clinton's events for free. I had heard that many wealthy progressives would do anything to get Bush out of the White House.

Many straightforward political donations, it had turned out, had been ineffective. It was 2002 and we had just come out of a disastrous mid-term election. These people would surely realize if they took back the media, they could make a difference. The one thing I did not take into consideration was human nature.

Man is driven to accumulate wealth and power. It's an evolutionary element of survival left by our reptilian predecessors. As Carl Sagan explains in *Dragons of Eden,* the source of this drive is located deep in the brain itself, in what has come to be called the Reptilian Complex. It is from here that the propensity arises for "aggressive behavior, territoriality, and the establishment of social hierarchies."

This remnant of our prehistoric past is concerned with survival, with getting and keeping food, and with facing danger—or fleeing from it. Our sense of power is determined by this ancient set of drives.

This drive is often indifferent to morality. We are wired by evolution to do things that have nothing to do with right or wrong. I believe the accumulation of wealth and power by the very few who succeed reflects this aspect of our evolutionary heritage; it's actually honored by the masses.

I have had the opportunity to meet and do business with some of the wealthiest people in the United States. Because of their wealth, they don't even need to make any investments at all. Jackie Mason has a great comeback to hecklers in his act. He says: "Mister, I don't care what you say because I have enough money to last the rest of my life." He continues, "unless I want to buy something." In the case of the wealthy, I've observed they have enough money to buy anything their heart desires—except immortality. Like the ancient Pharaohs, the wealthy try to create immortality and monuments to themselves in the form of legacies for their families. They usually fail because their descendents dissipate the family wealth by the third generation. Most of the rare exceptions occur when wealthy people create charitable foundations as Ford and Carnegie did.

Every year *Forbes Magazine* publishes a list of billionaires. Personally, I would be ashamed to be on that list. A billion dollars is a thousand times a million. How is it possible to justify the accumulation of such wealth when the vast majority of people are struggling or in abject poverty? How much is enough? Is ten million enough? One hundred million? What accounts for this desire to keep accumulating money? That is where the reptilian brain comes in, still compelling even the wealthiest of people to accumulate still more wealth and power. Let me give you an actual experience with one of my clients.

When I left the IRS in 1971 I started practicing accounting. One of my first clients was a new company that would ultimately become one of the largest manufacturer of bar code printers in the world. However, in 1971 the CEO was poor and always short of cash. He could not afford to pay my fees, but I still worked with him through his cash crunch because I recognized his company had enormous potential. As the company became more successful, this man had some free cash and was willing to make investments in various deals I introduced to him. At that time, even though he was not yet a multimillionaire, his risk tolerance was pretty high. In 1991 his company went public. He became an overnight mega-multimillionaire. I had known the man for over twenty years so I felt I could speak freely to him. After the public offering I still did work for the company, and helped him a great deal, giving him valuable tax and financial advice.

In 1994 I had a bad feeling about one of his money managers who controlled $40 million of his money. He seemed to me a little shady. This money manager was vetted by an organization called YPO, Young Presidents Organization, a distinguished international organization whose membership consisted of young CEOs. Still, there were certain things about this manager that made me suspicious after I visited his office in Beverly Hills. I immediately told my client to pull his money out of the fund even though the fund was nominally showing a healthy investment return of eleven percent. Reluctantly, my client took my advice and a year later *The Wall Street Journal* reported that this manager was indeed a fraud and had dissipated hundreds of millions of dollars from many wealthy individuals and their companies.

The day the story broke I called my client to get his reaction. To my surprise, he was not happy or grateful in the least. Apparently he was upset about the fact that I had identified a flaw in a decision he had made. He could not live with that. When I jokingly asked for a bonus for saving him $40 million, he took me seriously and became furious. He practically threw me out of his office What a reaction! I immediately recognized that the relationship would soon be over. I made the awful mistake of uncovering a flaw in the man's judgment—his misplaced trust in this money manager—and he could not live with that. He knew that many people in his company would remember his error as long as I was still associated with him and the company.

The more money he had, the more he needed total control and power. Within six months we mutually agreed to end the relationship.

As soon as large sums of money are involved, a whole different set of values comes into play, and those ancient drives start to work their magic.

Now that you know my experience with the psychology of money, you will get a good picture of what we were up against. Yes, we got a great launch from the *New York Times* article, but the challenge ahead was immense. We had to raise millions to carry us through the staffing process and support the payroll of talent and other employees. We also needed to convince radio station owners to carry our content—Not to mention we needed to convince Al Franken to come on board. Jon Sinton would take care of the last two items on our agenda. Anita and I were responsible for fundraising.

Our road show took us mainly to the east and west coasts where we had meetings with very wealthy people in the public and private sector. Since many of the rich liberals we met were used to giving away millions of dollars in campaign contributions, I thought that an investment in a liberal media company with a potential for appreciation would make the fundraising easy. Just the opposite happened. The fact that this project was an investment instead of a donation immediately signaled danger to our potential investors. It set in motion the old reptilian brains of these prospects.

Why? Because we were not asking for a donation. We didn't want free money. We wanted an investment. AnShell and the Paradigm Group were virtually unknown to the rich liberals. All they saw was people asking for an investment of capital—which for them, represented the potential to lose wealth and power. The fact that AnShell was a profit making entity, and not non-profit, raised doubts about what we were peddling. It didn't matter that donations are a giveaway with no hope of any return. It seems people would rather give money away than lose it.

I tried to explain to these people that they should think of this as a philanthropic venture capital investment which also had a possibility of a major return. In addition, if the investment failed, they could write it off for tax purposes. But that old reliable reptilian brain was set in motion. Most of the interested liberals we talked to thought in terms of money as the ultimate goal, rather than as a means to realize the ambition we shared—the ambition to change the discourse in this country. Looking back, it probably would have been easier to have made this a not-for-profit venture.

14

Meet the Radio Skeptics

The radio establishment too made it clear that AnShell had a difficult hill to climb in order to be successful. Clear Channel, Infinity, and ABC owned almost all the radio stations in the country. The likelihood was small that these companies would be easily convinced to give AnShell distribution in major cities—even for their underperforming stations. It was too risky. It would be easier to come up with another "Rush replica," as they had with Sean Hannity and Michael Savage, than try something untested and new.

After Anita appeared on C-SPAN's *Washington Journal* in the spring of 2003, Rush Limbaugh and Sean Hannity were strongly critical of her naiveté about getting on the air. On his show, Rush actually commented on Anita's appearance, referring to her as the "brains" of our operation. They were not completely wrong. They knew who controlled the radio stations, and accordingly, were rightfully skeptical about our chances. After all, Clear Channel was making a fortune on right wing talk show hosts, and they believed there was no liberal audience.

The media companies, on the other hand, had fallen in love with the story of AnShell and kept on reporting on our company, which meant they were eager to see us crumble; like vultures, the media thrives on reports of failure, death, and catastrophe. They are so addicted to reporting fiascos that they kept on watching and reporting on us, hoping we would give them the story they wanted. This was all to our advantage. Many major newspaper in the country had stories about us that they either reprinted from other sources, or had their own reporters write. International publications such as *The Guardian* were also picking up the story.

Nonetheless, as noted, we had a big problem convincing rich liberals that we could succeed, and this was no less true for liberals in the media business. Two individual who certainly understood our distribution problems were Norm Pattis and John Sykes. Sykes was the head of Infinity Broadcasting and a great supporter of Clinton and Gore. Pattis was the founder and chairman of Westwood One, a radio syndication and content company affiliated with Infinity. I did not know Pattis personally, but I knew he was one of the largest donors to the Clintons. He was also well known in Hollywood circles. Ironically, Westwood One was syndicating right wing talk hosts such as Laura Ingram and G. Gordon Liddy. Its management was even involved in convincing Clinton and other Democrats in Congress to support the Telecommunications Act of 1996.

Ostensibly, the Telecommunications Act was supposed to provide deregulation for the radio and television industry. Only a handful of Senators including Russ Feingold of Wisconsin who was the co-sponsor of the McCain/Feingold legislation on campaign finance reform, voted against the Telecommunications Act. He knew it would give media more power to drive still more advertising dollars into elections. Before the Act passed, a company could own no more that twenty AM and twenty FM stations nationwide. The Telecommunications Act allowed companies to own as many stations as they wanted nationwide, and up to eight stations in each market. The argument was that deregulation was always good. But only the big media giants who had lobbied for passage of this act were the beneficiaries. The act did nothing for American citizens, except limit their access to a genuine range of programming and opinion as big companies began to buy up stations.

Deregulation is a particularly Orwellian term that has been used to convince the public that a bad thing is really a good thing. Deregulation today is really *regulation* that helps the biggest companies in any industry. Look at what deregulation did to California, driving it into an energy crisis, and the role it played in the Enron scandal. Instead of increasing competition, deregulation actually creates barriers to entry.

The ability of a single company—Clear Channel, for example— to buy up as many radio stations as they wanted, is just a legal way of crushing competition. Clear Channel now has about 1,200 stations in the U.S. When companies are not regulated, monopolies develop. That's why we have anti-trust laws.

Nonetheless, major backers of the Democratic Party supported this legislation, knowing it would feather their nests, without any concern for the public good.

The Telecommunications Act had a negative effect on us as well; rather than helping the small player, it has only made things harder for new media companies. A particular side effect of this act was that that only a few media companies now have control of all the major radio stations in the country. To get our content syndicated on these stations, AnShell Media would have to deal almost exclusively with the major radio conglomerates who were already convinced that liberal talk radio would not work. Before 1996 there were hundreds of independent operators who would have wanted our content. Now we faced a skeptical and resistant market. We would have to prove there was money to be made in the business of liberal talk radio.

Despite the skepticism presented by many of the media articles throughout the spring of 2003 the AnShell story continued to be hot. At the same time, there was interest in the project former Vice President Al Gore was undertaking with an entrepreneur named Joel Hyatt to purchase a cable TV channel. Like Air America Radio,

Gore's concept would be an alternative to the conservative slant of channels like Fox News.

In her article "Will We See Gore TV?" of June 18, 2003, in *Time Magazine,* Karen Tumulty included some information about AnShell. "Gore has been helpful to Chicago venture capitalists Sheldon and Anita Drobny, who announced in February that they planned to fund a liberal radio network to counterbalance such conservative commentators as Rush Limbaugh. Several sources said Gore has helped introduce the Drobnys to such Hollywood political forces as producer-director Rob Reiner. Comedian Al Franken, author of the book *Rush Limbaugh is a Big Fat Idiot* is considering hosting a show on the Drobny's network and added that the couple has approached Gore to do regular essays. Anita Drobny declined to comment...."

I was impressed with the accuracy of Tumulty's story and wondered how she got that information. It made us realize that the world was watching us now and we really felt the pressure to deliver. By the early summer of 2003 we had made considerable progress in fundraising, staffing, and talent recruitment.

Given how much energy we had put into defining our liberal radio network's form, we realized our content had to be impeccable. We needed a very particular mix of qualities that would not be easy to find. We knew from past experience, and from observing the success of conservative shows, that being simply informative was not enough—we had to be enjoyable to listen to as well. We also needed people with activist credentials who were willing to risk failure and unapologetically represent the cause. Finally, we also needed people who had solid radio experience.

As for outlets, we were in talks with owners of independently owned "terrestrial" radio stations, as AM and FM broadcast radio is called, as compared to internet and satellite radio. We also were in negotiations with the stations XM Satellite Radio and Sirius Satellite Radio. Certain people were key in helping us with our efforts on all fronts.

For example, while we were visiting the studios of XM on one of our many trips to Washington, D.C., former President Bill Clinton called me to advise me on how to approach media owners and program directors. In my opinion, President Clinton was a model case of the damage media can do. The media affected his Presidency negatively, and he was very interested in changing the discourse. Lee Abrams, the program director for XM impatiently waited while I stayed on the phone for forty-five minutes. When I apologized and told him who was responsible for the interruption, he forgave my rudeness.

Both the Clintons and the Gores wanted us to succeed, and were helpful in giving us advice and making introductions. Al Gore was responsible for introducing us to John Sykes, the president of Infinity Broadcasting. Gore attended our meeting with Skyes in New York. Al Gore is a very astute person and was able, with nuance, to direct the meeting and shed a positive light on our radio concept. Sykes left the meeting with a favorable view of AnShell and our vision. Unfortunately, a deal never was forthcoming. Despite that, Al Gore gave us enormous credibility and did everything possible to help us, for which we were grateful.

The Clintons also helped us with important introductions to the institutional investors they knew. The meetings we scheduled with their help would make any investment banker jealous. We had the chance to meet top union and public state pension funds in the country. It was a dream list, and we have the Clintons to thank.

These meetings, along with the support of Clinton and Gore, gave Anita and me the confidence to believe that we would raise enough incremental money to get AnShell on the air. We knew our original estimate of $10 million would not be enough to pull off a launch of major talk radio network. But that summer brought everyone at AnShell hope that we would get our funding by September of 2003, which would let us sign talent and build the executive team and their staff in time for an early 2004 broadcast. The election year was an important year to be on the air for a network advocating the position of the "loyal opposition."

By midsummer we had raised about $2 million from our own sources at the Paradigm Group. We had tentative commitments of millions more from larger institutional investors. The problem with the larger institutional investors was that none of them ever wants to invest alone. We had commitments of at least $100 million from this group if only we could find one who would invest first.

We finally found one labor union who loved our plan, and made a tentative commitment of $50 million, via their president, treasurer, and political director. All that remained was their due diligence—a process of evaluating the validity of claims made in a business plan either directly or through third party research. This process is done by a financial advisor.

Since we knew our business plan was good and had the support of the top brass of the union, we concluded that our funding was assured. We then began to focus more on the Franken contract and other talent such as Janeane Garofalo and Mike Malloy.

The business plan was sent to the union's financial advisor, who had contracted an outside consulting firm to do the due diligence. In early July of 2003 we scheduled a meeting with him. We expected the due diligence to take no more than thirty days. We were so close to $50 million we could taste it.

15

Just Say Yes

The summer of 2003 unfolded slowly as we found ourselves waiting for that elusive "yes." While we were waiting for a response from the union, we decided we had nothing to lose by trying to raise money from other groups.

After thirty days we had still not heard from the union's financial advisor. Javier called him. He told Javier that he was still awaiting the due diligence requests that had been promised by union leaders. He said he was very busy and apologized for his delay, and he assured Javier he would get in contact with the outside advisory firm, and move the process along.

The next day Javier came into my office with a perplexed look on his face. Javier Saade is a seasoned financial professional with over ten years of experience with McKinsey and Abbott Labs, among other companies. He knew how to handle due diligence requests. The perplexed look came from the fact that the so-called financial advisory firm had assigned an intern to the due diligence of AnShell. The kid had just graduated from college with a degree in psychology. What in the world was going on? I decided to do a "Google" search of this advisory firm.

I discovered that the firm was a small, inexperienced group staffed with political cronies of a national political figure. The group had enough clout to become trustees on state and local pension funds. The man in charge of the due diligence—the one who handed the project off to a psychology major intern—was a lawyer who had no business degree. His big credential was that he was close to the afore-mentioned politico who had opened the door for him to be a trustee of a county pension fund—a scandalous kind of cronyism since appointees are responsible for managing billions of dollars.

I got in touch with the union financial advisor and asked him what was going on. Right away I knew something was wrong. In a perfectly polite conversation he proceeded to tell me that if we could find another investor, he might be inclined to make a favorable decision.

At least I knew exactly where I stood: the due diligence was being handled poorly at best, the staff—judging by the youth he had put in charge—seemed incompetent, and everything was moving in slow motion. As a result of this conversation, it became very important that we encourage other interested groups to speed up their process. I told Javier to call other investment groups and see if they might be interested in a meeting with this financial advisor.

It was now early August. Al Franken had finished his book, and was ready to start negotiating seriously. We had already hired top management people with radio experience, and our monthly "burn rate" would soon be at one million dollars by the end of September. We were starting to get desperate. The burden of the responsibility of getting this network on the air weighed heavily on Anita and me. The summer was almost over and we were no closer to the financing we so desperately needed. We needed a co-investor to take to the union and we needed one fast.

John Podesta had introduced us to David Goodfriend, a former Clinton aide, who was interested in the concept of AnShell Media.

Aware that we were raising money for a liberal radio network, Goodfriend arranged for us to meet an interested group of radio entrepreneurs. At this point, Javier and Jon were spearheading fundraising efforts for AnShell and the plan was they would bring Anita and me in when a solid deal was presented. On August 26, 2003, the interested party put an offer on the table.

We rejected it outright. They had offered us a small upfront payment and a small equity in their new company. We had come to the table with a solid business plan, a proven management team, and superb talent relationships—all of which were valuable. I didn't want to sell AnShell short. Not only that, we were looking for investors not buyers. But at the same time, we could go no further without money, and we wanted to see our concept for a liberal radio network succeed. Discussions continued in hopes that we would get a better offer. In October 2003 we reconvened.

This time Anita and I were willing to accept their offer. It was our turn to do our due diligence on the interested party. Since they purported to have enough capital to fund AnShell Media, we weren't surprised when we saw that the group owned radio stations overseas and had cash holdings worth millions of dollars. They had built a series of small advertising firms in the Pacific, merged them together, sold them to a big ad agency and made a fortune from it. According to our due diligence in October 2003, the group had the financial resources to bring our liberal radio network to life. However, we would have to sell the company and give up almost all of the equity. That was their terms. We accepted the offer. The group of radio entrepreneurs was officially "The Buyers."

By the way, returning to our friends at the union—before we had a deal with The Buyers, we thought we had had, at the very least, a potential co-investor in this group of radio entrepreneurs. In mid-August I sent one of the buyers to the union. If they could work things out, together we might be able to move forward. If the union liked what they saw, AnShell would have 50 million dollars and new partners. Unfortunately, the union advisor liked what he saw so much, he made a separate deal with The Buyers, and cut us out completely. The union agreed to provide over $35 million as a line of credit for The Buyers to purchase radio stations in the future. The Reptilian Complex had done its work again. As it turned out, The Buyer never acquired any radio stations and the line of credit was never used.

16

Air America Takes Off

The following month was a transitional phase. With our blessing, Jon Sinton and Javier Saade joined The Buyers in their new company. On November 17, 2003, the deal was closed. Suddenly Anita and I were out of the picture.

In one of our meetings, The Buyers had introduced us to Mark Walsh, a leading contender for the CEO position if the new company were to prevail. Walsh is a former America Online executive and ran an e-commerce site called Verticalnet Inc., which once reached a peak value of $12.4 billion during the heady dot.com days. At least we were comforted that Mark Walsh, Javier Saade, and Jon Sinton were going to be part of the new management team.

On November 17 AnShell Media became Air America Radio. The Buyers came up with the name after discussion with a public relations firm. The Buyers formed a holding company called Progress Media. Progress Media, in turn, owned two companies: Air America Radio was the content company, and the second one was Equal Time, which would buy radio stations that would broadcast Air America.

After the company transferred ownership, The Buyers and their management team took our concept, rewrote the business plan and went to work. From a distance, we watched as the new management set up shop.

They spent a lot of time in discussions with radio groups to see if they would be interested in partnering with their new radio network. At this point in time it was less about money-raising and more about executing the idea. They started to hire the talent for different shows, signed on writers and producers, brought in a controller, set up benefits, and partnered with a lawyer to help with negotiations. They opened new offices on lower Park Avenue. Air America first secured distribution with Inner City Broadcasting Corporation, who agreed to lease stations to Air America in San Francisco, the fourth largest market, and New York, the number one market.

In addition to building the company, The Buyers also continued down the fundraising road. They still needed a lot more capital to meet the hefty business plan.

David Goodfriend, Mark Walsh, and Javier Saade represented Air America at many fundraising events. The trio made presentations in front of the Hollywood personalities like Norman and Lynn Lear, Larry and Laurie David, Stanley Bing—a major contributor to the Democratic National Committee—Warren Beatty, and others. Everyone loved the idea and verbally committed money, but it didn't mean they wrote the checks. Again, these potential investors wanted proof that their money was being well invested, and they insisted on knowing whether there were other investors who had already put money in Air America. It was a kind of Catch-22; everyone wanted to put in money, but only if someone else put it in first.

Goodfriend, Walsh, and Saade also started firming up details with Al Franken's agent at William Morris, Henry Reisch. By January 6, 2004, they had locked in a deal. The agreement was contingent on the condition Air America would let Franken hire his own team of writers and researchers. Air America also made a commitment to get Franken's show heard in the top three markets in the US by March 31. This made March 31 the "drop dead date" Air America Radio had to be on the air.

At this point, The Buyers already had the first and fourth markets taken care of with Inner City Broadcasting Corporation, but that still left Los Angeles and Chicago—the number two and three markets. If Air America didn't get those two markets by March 31, the deal with Franken was off.

The new team was obsessed with finding workable media outlets. They negotiated with one group after another to get coverage in Los Angeles and Chicago. They had no choice; Al Franken was a key component in the talent line-up and these were the terms.

Meanwhile, things were not off to a smooth start in the new company. People did not trust each other and there seemed to be a lot of infighting among staff. Financially, too, things were simply not working right. Air America started missing bills, and checks were bouncing.

In late January of 2004 there was an emergency management staff meeting. In a large company, it's difficult to have an all-management staff meeting on a weekly basis, but in a small company, like Air America, it is simply good business sense to hold weekly staff meetings to ensure everyone's goals and objectives are aligned. But the January meeting was the last all-management staff meeting. The Buyers tended to meet with different groups within the company. People went away with conflicting views of where the company was going.

To insiders, Air America's programming department did not appear all that well-organized. One person was in charge of news, another was in charge of comedy, and somebody else was head of commentary, with no one as captain of the ship. Each person was gunning for the same top programming job. People were getting in each other's way and senior management couldn't help because they themselves were in the dark.

Though Mark Walsh was CEO—and an incredibly capable one at that—as the March 31 deadline approached, he did not have full access to company finances, nor did he seem fully in charge. While Air America was meeting performance benchmarks and receiving tons of media attention, inside the walls all was not well.

17

In the Spotlight

Anita and I had been going about our daily business in the months leading up to Air America's launch. In spite of our role as founders, we were isolated from the operations. We were busy with other projects, and getting increasingly involved in politics at a national level. We had the opportunity to meet the major 2004 Democratic presidential candidates and their advisors. It was ironic that in 2004 many of them were trying to raise money from us for their campaigns, just as we had earlier been trying to get help from them. We had met with Howard Dean in Chicago in the early spring of 2003 when his campaign was hot. We had also met with John Edwards in Chicago to try to get help from the Trial Lawyers Association. Anita met with John Kerry while she was in DC. All of them had been interested in seeing our project take off in time for the 2004 campaign and election.

But even as we were swept up in national politics, Anita and I read, watched and listened to the media about Air America Radio. Jon Sinton and Mark Walsh were quoted everywhere. Mark Walsh, in an online question and answer session with *The Washington Post,* summed up Air America's agenda: "Our goal is to entertain and inform. We are capitalists and want to build a profitable business.

We believe radio is an emotional, passionate and message-friendly medium. We hope we arouse the same passions in our listeners as successful talk show hosts who've preceded us have done in theirs."

In the days leading up to the launch, Air America was covered in *Newsweek, Variety, BusinessWeek, USA Today, Time,* as well as overseas coverage in Australia, the UK, and India. Air America got about $12 million worth of earned media or free advertising. From *Nightline* to the *Today Show,* the network was in the news.

Air America's talent, accustomed to being in the public eye, also was also out there laying the groundwork and setting the tone for what would be coming. Janeane Gorofalo, extolling the virtues of a radio network with a left-leaning view, told USA reporter, Peter Johnson, on March 29, only a few days before Air America started broadcasting, "Over the past 30 years the American people have been conned into thinking "liberal" is a dirty word. Because of liberal reforms, we enjoy things like desegregation, child labor laws, environmental protection, seat belts and birth control. These are liberal reforms that we as a contemporary culture brag about, take for granted and enjoy, so how is it that liberalism is a dirty word?"

Radio establishment coverage from places like *Radio Business Report* and *Talkers* was skeptical, and there was no shortage of published opinion that said Air America will never get off the ground. And there was also plenty of free press from the right. One story written by Byron York for the *National Review* was particularly revealing of the way conservative media handles the competition.

This article was one of the earlier stories that covered Air America, and it appeared in the October 27, 2003 issue of the *National Review.* The title was "Liberal Radio and Its Dark Angel, Meet the Amazing Sheldon Drobny." My first contact with Byron York was by email. He sent me a request for information on September 29, 2003. In that request, he asked for information about some of my writings on a progressive web site called makethemaccountable.com. This is a site run by my good friend and associate, Carolyn Kay, who had been working with me almost from the beginning of the formation of Air America.

I knew that if I agreed to talk to Byron, any article he would write about me would not be complimentary. I decided to give him a full interview on the record. Actually, I was doing an experiment about how the right wing would report on our network. I wanted to see whether he would skew the story his own way if I went on the record with him. I thought I had nothing to lose since being trashed by the right wing would be sort of a badge of courage.

I happen to like Byron York. Nonetheless, his article would most likely be reflective of the political positions of his publisher the *National Review*. The next week, as agreed, York interviewed me.

He asked me a number of questions about our radio network, but seemed to be more interested in the articles I had written for makethemaccountable.com. He focused on two articles I wrote with the following admittedly-provocative quotes. In the first one I claimed, "GE, News Corporation, and Richard Mellon Scaife essentially dictate what the government does in a process that is quasi-fascist." I went on to say, "... the corporate masters and their current spokesman, George W. Bush ... use the same excuses Hitler used to sell the public his maniacal desire to conquer Europe." He also asked about this quote: "Nazi Germany's military industrial complex allowed it to rearm and start a second world war. Much of the support for Germany's rearmament came from American and international businesses, a scandal that has never been completely made public. Very few Americans know that Prescott Bush, our President's grandfather, supplied Nazi Germany with such assistance ... President Roosevelt, in 1942, froze some of his assets under the Trading With The Enemies Act." Byron was particularly interested in the last quote.

The first two quotes were clearly just my opinion but the last one was not. In fact, Prescott Bush and G. Roland Harriman, a Democrat, were directors and owners of a company that traded with Nazi Germany, and had had its assets frozen. Byron seemed surprised at this fact and asked for my source. I told him to just look on the internet. He could have easily found the sources himself because a reporter named John Buchanan had broken the story in the *New Hampshire Gazette* the previous August as a result of a release of declassified information from The National Archives. However, Byron insisted I send him examples of those sources. I sent York the Buchanan article and three others I picked at random.

One of the sources was from a book called *George Bush: The Unauthorized Biography,* written by two people who were supporters of Lyndon LaRouche. LaRouche is considered a less than credible political figure. Sure enough, York chose to report on the least credible source of the four I sent, in his article about me.

After I read the article in the *National Review,* I called York just for fun, to ask him why he didn't mention the other, more reputable articles I had sent. He didn't have a particularly good answer but agreed to allow me an editorial reply, included here in the appendix.

A few weeks later, after the Chicago Cubs broke my heart and lost the playoff series with the Florida Marlins, I asked a friend to help me publish a letter to the editor criticizing Fox Sports' unfair coverage against the Cubs. I wanted to express my opinion that they had a biased, second rate broadcasting team working for them. One of sportscasters had been fired as a broadcaster for the Cubs, and the other two had played for their opposition in the playoffs. I got the letter published as a "Featured Letter" in the *Chicago Sun-Times* on October 20, 2003. The next day I got a call from Fox News asking for a picture of me for an interview by Brit Hume with Byron York the following day. I suspected Fox wanted to get even with me for trashing their coverage of the Cubs.

The next day Anita and I watched *Special Report* with Brit Hume and got an example of Fox's concept of "fair and balanced reporting," to borrow their phrase. The initial part of the interview with York was complimentary to me and there was also a discussion of our radio project. At that time, York was not aware of our sale of AnShell to the group we've been calling The Buyers.

After this, the interview focused on my writings and how far on the fringe my opinions were for a so-called "rich capitalist." They proceeded to discuss the Bush/Nazi story, focusing on the LaRouche related sources in order to convince their audience that the story had no credibility. Both Hume and York had to know that the story was accurate, yet all the other sources including the National Archives release were not mentioned.

This experience provided a very telling point about the power of the media in this country; if they want to marginalize you, they will slant the story any way they can.

Our hope for Air America Radio was that it would create a balance to this distortion. Although we wanted the network to be entertaining and funny, we never wanted to be accused of lying. If we did that, we would have only succeeded in turning talk radio into the equivalent of World Federation Wrestling.

Most of all, we wanted to set an example of how a media company can make money by telling the truth. As Jon Sinton says, "Our vision was simply to balance the discourse because I think for democracy to function properly, it needs an informed electorate." The creative vision behind Air America is driven by a desire to broaden the discourse in a way that will support democracy—not tear it down even further.

Sometimes the issue is not even dishonesty as much as a dumbing down of the discourse. The problem I have is with the way the corporate media focuses on the most shallow aspect of any issue.

For example, I think that Chris Matthews of the MSNBC program *Hardball* is an intelligent and entertaining political analyst. The key to his show, however, has always been entertainment at the expense of real analysis. This became especially clear recently at the 2004 Democratic Convention when Bill Clinton gave his address. Matthews has no interest in analyzing issues. He and his panel of political analysts reviewed the political players as if they were actors on a stage. Instead of discussing the content of Clinton's speech, the

Hardball group discussed Clinton's performance only. Clinton is a fine orator who captivates audiences. But so were FDR and Churchill. Could you imagine Edward R. Morrow or Walter Cronkite discussing the performance and not the content of the speeches of FDR? That is what our media has done to the political process in this country.

The *Hardball* group seemed obsessed with "the cultural divisions" between the two parties, but never talked about the details of those divisions. When Clinton addressed these so-called cultural divisions in his speech, suggesting they were a myth created by the Republicans to divide and conquer, the analysts were not interested.

This lack of substance was not just reserved for Clinton. When President Carter addressed the Convention, Matthews appeared shocked that this mild mannered former President had the audacity to say that this nation is being intentionally scared by the Bush administration. I do not know where Matthews has been living since the 2000 election, but a hallmark of the Bush administration has been its fixation on evil, which they see everywhere—potentially in every citizen. How could he not know, that one of the keys to the Bush administration, with its ambiguous amber alerts, has been fear? Mathews is not into analysis based on the facts; rather he, and so many others are interested only in the surface.

There's nothing wrong with entertainment. But it doesn't have to come at the expense of the truth.

18

The Mad Dash

Bad management and loose financial controls aside, as it approached launch day, Air America was growing at an exponential rate. It went from a five person company in November of 2003, to a ten person company by the end of the year, to twenty-five people at the end of January '04. The company doubled in size in February, and again in March of '04 when it had one hundred people working for it.

In November 2003 it cost Air America $200,000 a month to operate. When the station launched in March, the company was burning up somewhere between $1.5 million to $2 million dollars per month.

Mark Walsh was the man The Buyers put in charge of this expanding operation. As CEO of Air America, Mark Walsh had found a job that suited him perfectly; it was the ideal balance between Mark's professional expertise and his political activities. Aside from his impressive background as an executive for companies like AOL, HBO and Verticalnet, Mark was also chief Internet adviser for the Democratic National Committee, and briefly served the same role for the John Kerry presidential campaign. Air America was Mark's chance to help get a liberal voice on America's radio airwaves, and if there was anyone capable of making that happen, it was Mark.

It didn't happen. As noted, Mark was never given the tools to make Air America Radio fly. Says Javier Saade, then Executive Vice President, "As CEO, Mark should have had much more control over the finances. He was never given full reign of the company." As CFO, Javier himself should have been involved in overseeing company expenses—something that also never happened. The Buyers kept a tight grip on their control over Air America's finances, and senior management was kept in the dark about the company's true financial status.

It turns out the buyers had been as unsuccessful as we were at raising money from what I call the "the limousine liberals." Though they thought they could do a better job of raising money from this group, they faced the same difficulties we did; it was too risky an investment for most people's taste.

Air America was running out of money, and The Buyers naturally kept their CEO and CFO in the dark about the growing cash flow shortage. This is not untypical in business; it is often a good idea to keep management in the dark about cash requirements if one believes that money will be coming shortly. There's no point in causing unnecessary insecurity in top management with financial worries.

Problems don't just disappear, however, and things got so bad, that in an email memo to The Buyers, written in March 2004, Javier warned, "The company is in horrible shape. Its organizational structure, support functions, employee productivity and financial prospects are dire. Radical and immediate steps are necessary." He could not have been any clearer.

Air America was on a spending spree, hiring lawyers, advertising agencies, public relations firms, design firms, and many other vendors. Bills from these vendors started to come in but the money to pay them wasn't going out. Observing the company's unpaid bills, Javier started questioning The Buyers' financial standing.

Initially Javier told himself the financial problems were nothing unusual; it was just a small company's way of trying to preserve cash and stretch out payments. He never even saw the financials. But when a barrage of twenty vendors came knocking on the door claiming they had never been paid, Javier knew there was a problem. This problem even found its way into a *Wall Street Journal* article which reported Air America's "former Los Angeles market manager says he discovered in March the company hadn't paid the rent on its office there. In April vendors stopped delivering office supplies because they weren't getting paid and contractors, such as electricians, complained that their checks weren't arriving."

On March 19, 2004, desperate to get his hands on some cash, CEO Mark Walsh asked The Buyers for a list of the investors they had solicited in the past couple months. "Is there a file with the actual names, numbers and addresses?" he asked. Mark wanted to check whether he could use their names in speaking to other constituencies as he went about fundraising. Mark was not asking for something out of the ordinary—this is a standard practice when raising capital. In fact, an Excel spreadsheet with names, numbers and addresses of potential investors is the norm. Mark never got a response.

Meanwhile, Air America Radio executives were still working frantically to secure the two markets they needed most—Chicago and Los Angeles—in order to guarantee Al Franken's participation. Air America Radio had so far been unsuccessful at purchasing stations in these cities. The only other alternative was to lease stations.

The most readily available stations in these cities belonged to Arthur Lui, owner of Multicultural Radio Broadcasting, Inc. In a rush not to lose out, The Buyers cut one of the worst deals imaginable. Multicultural was a great option from a station perspective, but from a financial perspective it was a disaster. In LA alone, the total bill for the year was going to be north of $4 million. By comparison, if Air America had waited only a few more weeks, Javier could have closed another deal he was spearheading, to buy an AM radio outlet in Los Angeles. That would have cost about

$1.5 million—$2.5 million less per year. Air America's already precarious financial standing worsened.

As per their agreement, The Buyers took control of Arthur Lui's stations in LA and Chicago in February of 2004. They ran free Hispanic programming until their launch date of March 31.

March was a mad dash to get everything into place for the launch. The Buyers had to build their sales teams in different markets. Creatives had to write and produce programming skits and content. The technical team had to get all the engineering aspects of the station up and running, and replace antiquated broadcasting equipment. Each of these tasks cost money. The pressure on the staff was immense. "In a month we got this thing up and running," says Javier. "It was insane, we were working twenty hour days, seven days a week. The atmosphere was rough but also collegial because everyone was focused on the goal. But it was brutal. By the point of launching, we had 700 skits, which is unheard of."

Besides the technical set up, they had to train people how to do radio, since many of the people they had hired had never been on the air.

Air America's talent and content had been in the works for several months, led by John Sinton. "We were looking for people who could be credible spokespersons for the left." Jon and three other members of Air America's staff were more or less responsible for content. "Shelly Lewis, who is Vice President of Programming in Charge of Content, really built the infrastructure. She hired producers and bookers," says Sinton, describing the process. "She was a former producer at CNN and Good Morning America. Lizz Winstead, who was the co-creator of *The Daily Show,* is the creative soul of the network. And Dave Logan, Executive Vice President of Programming, was the first guy we hired. He had a phenomenal background and was one of the best known programmers in the country. The four of us sat in a room and we ate and listened to a lot of tapes. It's a process."

Some of their choices—besides the more high profile talent like Franken and Gorofalo who they had met through AnShell—included Mark Riley who had been with WLIB before Air America took over. WLIB was a local New York radio station serving the black and Caribbean community for many years. Mark Riley was slated to co-host *Morning Sedition* with Marc Maron, a comedian and cultural critic. Mike Malloy, one of our original choices, also remained on the talent roster, though he was not part of our launch. And Chuck D, the outspoken rapper behind Public Enemy brought an original point of view and a highly recognizable presence. He would join Lizz Winstead and Rachel Maddow on the show, *Unfiltered*.

Even as Air America approached its March 31 launch date, the company's image was sparkling to the outside world. The launch date was promoted everywhere, and a huge party was planned in an ultra-hip, downtown New York hotel.

By this time, Anita and I were only a memory to the Air America staff—at least to those who even knew us. The company we had conceived now had nothing to do with us. This became painfully apparent when we were not invited to the Air America launch party on March 30. Javier was in charge of organizing the party. He says Anita and I were the first people on his invitee list. But it seems someone didn't want us there and we were taken off the list.

The party was an extravagant affair that left little doubt that liberals are as good at hearty self-indulgence as the conservatives are. It took place at a hip new hotel called the Maritime, between Chelsea and the Meat Packing district in Manhattan. The bash reputedly cost $70,000. The place was packed and everyone on the staff was there except Dave Logan who was back at the studios making sure the equipment was up and running.

Enjoying the red, white, and blue cocktails were guests, media, supporters, and some of New York's outspoken actors and musicians who are high profile supporters of the liberal cause. As Jon Sinton describes the party, "It was a loud, raucous evening of the dawn of a new day. The atmosphere was electric."

With the exception of the Air America launch the next day, that was the last time the staff would be smiling for quite a while.

19

First, the Good News

At 12 P.M. on March 31, 2004, America's first liberal radio network went on the air, broadcasting from New York City. It also went on the air in Los Angeles and Chicago and several smaller markets.

Everyone on the staff was there, although most people listened to the broadcast from offices on the other floors occupied by Air America; it was impossible to get near the studio. Reporters were literally tangled up in each other's cables. You'd step around the camera of a CNN correspondent, bump into someone from the *New York Times,* then step around them and trip over a Fox Network cable. It was a mob scene.

Al's first day on the radio was off to a respectable, if not perfect start. His first solid three hours in radio had both high and low points, as is to be expected. Michael Moore and former Senator Bob Kerrey joined him as a guest, and former Vice President Al Gore called in. Randi Rhodes got in a screaming match with Ralph Nadar. There were also call-ins from "the other side" in the form of Pat Buchanan and G. Gordon Liddy. Variety called it "an awkward affair," but just as many listeners found it to be a good first step towards just what we intended: "lively, smart and surprisingly energetic radio."

The staff wasn't sure if the whole thing was even going to work—they had a huge amount of brand new equipment that had never been tested. As noted, Dave Logan had spent the entire night before making sure he knew how to work each piece of equipment. There were glitches with the LA broadcast, but Chicago and New York went well, and the staff broke out some well-deserved champagne.

Two days after Air America's highly publicized launch and the media fanfare that surrounded it, the company's executives were again facing problems. Things were getting worse. On April 2, Dave Logan, Executive Vice President of Programming and Operations, was exasperated by problems with Air America's computer systems—or the lack of them. He was understaffed and overstressed. He sent a memo venting his frustration. After outlining five critical steps Air America needed to take immediately in order to compensate for these shortcomings, Dave concluded, "We are under-equipped for our current needs and barely scraping by behind the scenes. The magic touch will eventually fade. We got it on and had a great time doing it. Now we need to keep the system running right so it can support our business product. We're in the big leagues now and we have to compete like we belong there."

When Mark Walsh brought Dave's memo to the Buyers, he was assured everything was already taken care of. But the problems came crashing down at the end of April as reality caught up with Air America Radio. After only two weeks on the air, the LA and Chicago stations had been turned off. It took a while for people like Mark and Javier to figure out what had happened.

Apparently, The Buyers claimed Arthur Lui's Multicultural Radio owed them money. During February and March, when Air America was not yet on the air, Hispanic programming had been running on both the LA and Chicago stations. The Buyers had made an agreement with Multicultural, that Air America and Multicultural would split any operating profit made in those two months. But no significant revenues were produced because this programming was broadcast for free. Multicultural Radio claimed they didn't owe Air America anything.

Air America fought back against Multicultural, and they filed a suit in New York State Supreme Court to get the station back on the air. The judge ordered Air America temporarily back on the air but much damage was done.

The disaster grew. Staff wasn't being paid. The talent was vocally in revolt. Checks were bouncing left and right. The public perception of Air America Radio was in disarray, and there was gossip that Air America was about to shut down.

The commentary in the ever-observant press was downright gleeful at times. The May 7 edition of *Radio Business Report,* said in their Radio News column, "Tire pressure is so low inside Air America it has and most likely will continue to hit these speed bumps and hard. Hate to be sitting on the passenger side or the back of this bus when they hit [a] Pittsburgh pothole." An article in *Broadcasting & Cable* on April 19, written by Pulitzer Prize-winning journalist Howard Rosenberg, started off, "Free at last, free at last. Or maybe not, with newborn Air America radio last week tripping over its own umbilical cord by getting flushed, at least temporarily, from the airwaves in Los Angeles and Chicago in a murky dispute over money."

The problems began to take its toll on senior management. Mark Walsh resigned in late April. Javier left shortly thereafter. Things were falling apart, and neither Mark nor Javier felt they had the power do anything about it.

It was only a couple days later, on May 5, that we got the auspicious call from Doug Kreeger. He informed Anita and me that the company was hanging on by a thread.

20

Conference Room Confidential

After two years of hard labor it had all come to this: Air America Radio's Chicago station was broadcasting in Spanish, off the air in Los Angeles, an object of derision for the smug doomsday prophets on the right, and—as Doug Kreeger had put it—hanging by a thread. Which brings us back to that early May day in 2004 when we appeared in New York City at an emergency meeting of all of Air America's investors.

After Doug called us we flew to New York City and went straight to Air America Offices on Park Avenue, joining other investors who had already gathered there.

Javier Saade greeted us when we arrived. He appeared to be on the verge of a breakdown. Javier proceeded to tell us Air America had millions of dollars of unpaid bills. There was no money left for the current payroll, and employee health insurance bills hadn't been paid. I tried to calm him down, jokingly asking, "Other than that everything is OK, right?" He did not laugh.

The room was small and hot. We felt like sardines stuffed in a hot can. There were no food or beverages because every spare inch of space was reserved for people. Besides the remaining management team, the room was packed with Air America's now very angry investors.

Regarding these investors, while no one had succeeded in bringing America's more outspoken "limousine liberals" on board, The Buyers had managed to bring in new and important investors. They came from a range of backgrounds, and included people who invested in Air America for political reasons as well as those who simply thought it was a sound investment.

Javier, like everyone else in the room, was distraught. To lift his spirits, I then told Javier something I had told Anita on the flight to New York, something we could prove by just looking around the room—this time we were not alone. Anita and I were not the only investors anymore. The people in this room had a combined net worth of at least a billion dollars. If we could calm them down and focus on our objectives, we could solve this crisis and move forward. We only had to reassure investors that everything was going to be all right.

Various people spoke that evening, including me, and many of the investors got to speak their minds as well. I shared the reorganization plan we had developed that would hopefully save the company. The implementation of the plan was going to take the full cooperation of the investors, creditors, employees, and talent. In addition, we needed to get our attorneys engaged by the group as a whole, without creating a feeling of paranoia from the other investors. Our attorney, Rick Bernthal, had a good relationship with the owners of our flagship station, WLIB, in New York and their cooperation was necessary to keep Air America Radio alive. What started off as a furious confrontation ended with high hopes.

Anita was instrumental in that process that day. I have said Anita was the mother of this project; in fact, her friends affectionately call her "earth mother." She's fair, her intentions are always sincere, and she has the inner strength to persevere in situations much like the one we faced in the conference room that day. I often tease here about being super human since she appears to be devoid of what, in biblical terms, is called "the evil inclination." Anita also has a wonderful capability to lead and control a meeting—

especially those meetings of men with large egos and loads of testosterone who are watching a fortune run down the drain.

All of the investors in the room that day wanted to save Air America, and each for his or her own reason. One investor, for example, was not political at all, but simply thought the business plan was a winner. When the meeting ended, Anita and I knew we had our work cut out for us in order to implement the reorganization plan. We knew that there were many pieces that had to work together in order for the reorganization to be successful. At least this group of investors, talent, and employees all desperately wanted Air America Radio to succeed. That was the major advantage of this difficult situation. When diverse interests collectively want something to work, almost anything can be achieved. That was the light we all saw at the end of the meeting.

21

Facing the Future

In a reorganization, the usual procedure for paying old bills is to get an agreed upon payment plan from old creditors to address past due bills, and keep current on new bills. From a past due creditor's point of view, this is a reasonable alternative. If a past due creditor doesn't agree to a payment plan and a company goes under, the creditors are stuck with lost revenue which they must write off, and they lose any potential new business. Air America's past due creditors were motivated to stay on board.

As for Air America's employees, I suggested a furlough for some employees until we got our funding in order. We very much tried to be fair to all the innocent victims of past mismanagement. We also suggested a 25% salary deferral across the board to be repaid when we got our funding.

We offered both creditors and employees equity in the new company we had formed, Piquant, in lieu of payment. This is something McDonald's did in their early days, that ultimately made millionaires out of those employees who could not be paid in cash. It was a solid reorganization plan, right out of the MBA textbook at Harvard.

We were anxious to be fair to the old creditors, employees, and talent and we were willing to spend the money to make it work. Normally in a reorganization, payments to the old creditors are delayed; in our case, the board has been generous to everyone and has tried to satisfy all participants. Almost everyone stayed with the company. The implementation of the reorganization plan has not been easy but the plan seems to be working.

The final Arbitron ratings for April through June arrived in July of 2004, and our New York ratings looked terrific, as did the ratings from our affiliates around the country. They showed Al Franken actually beating his nemesis, Bill O' Reilly, in the coveted 25-54 age range. The hits on the Internet at airamericaradio.com were about 2,000,000 a week, thanks to so much media publicity—both good and bad. More affiliates are knocking on the door.

The importance of Air America's success lies in the fact that it has demonstrated there is indeed a place in the world for liberal radio network. Jon Sinton was right when he said to me almost two years ago, when we first got started, that Air America was going to be bigger than all of us. As Jon observed recently, "Whether Air America stays around or not, the concept of liberal radio has been validated."

The problems Air America Radio faced are typical of the early days of any new and struggling company that ultimately has a chance to grow. As a venture capitalist, I have witnessed many similar startup problems that had to be overcome before success was achieved. The difference is that Air America's story took place in a proverbial fishbowl for all the world to see—after all, it was a media story.

When *The Wall Street Journal* called me in June, for example, about a front-page story they were doing about Air America, we all said no. It was too soon after our reorganization and I didn't want this part of our story to be public. This was a mistake. When you say nothing to reporters, they get the story from the outside.

Considering our recent history and clash with The Buyers, that could only be bad news.

The day the *Wall Street Journal* article was published, I got hundreds of calls asking if we were still in business. This was at a time when we were once again aggressively raising money. A front page *Wall Street Journal* story that aired our dirty laundry was not very helpful. But that's part of being in the public eye; you don't have total control over what's said about you. You just have to keep moving forward and do what you believe in.

A dramatic change has taken place in the business of mass media in recent years. News has become entertainment, and the newsroom, a profit center. Anything of real substance rarely makes a dent in the news these days while minor, sensational conflicts—salacious crimes, phony conflicts, and gossip—take up valuable time and space. The corporate-owned media will do anything to avoid the real, difficult issues if they can keep listeners addicted to mindless trash, and get better ratings in the process. Nonetheless, we have a public aching to be informed, and hungering for an alternative. The audience is there, and Air America is trying to capture the moment. I predict Air America Radio will be just the first of many media outlets to tap this audience.

Today, Air America Radio is managed by a fine group of experienced radio executives. Many of the original staff members are still on board. Jon Sinton is President, Doug Kreeger is CEO, and Carl Ginsburg, a highly honored producer and journalist, is Chief Operating Officer. There's a nine person board, and each of the members is also an investor. They are a very impressive group indeed, from a variety of backgrounds. Anita is the vice-chairperson and the only woman on the board. The Paradigm Group is still investors, but we are not involved in the day to day operations of Air America.

Jon Sinton, of all the participants in the Air America story, has been there longest and his enthusiasm remains undiminished. "I've been doing this a long time. I suspected we had a hit. But it's been bigger, faster than I thought it would be," he says, adding, "Who knows what tomorrow will bring."

Our flagship station, WLIB in New York City, is climbing in the ratings. In the 18–34 age range category for talk radio, we are ahead of the competition—WOR and WABC—in almost every time slot. Although we have time before we pull ahead of Rush, I'm confident we'll get there. You can now get into a taxi cab in New York City and hear Air America on the car radio instead of the usual suspects. The word is spreading. The audience of Air America is choice for advertisers, with talk radio the most profitable part of the radio business. Now many station owners who watched in envy as conservative radio stations reaped enormous profits, have a chance to enter that market as well with liberal talk programming. Previously, it was believed that Rush and the other conservative talk shows were the only game in talk radio. Given the opportunity to participate in a new market, the pathway has been cleared for many under performing stations in other major cities to get on board.

Air America Radio is adding markets exponentially; just recently Denver and Philadelphia joined Air America Radio's affiliates. Air America's coverage now reaches 25% of the country. Affiliates are coming on board almost weekly, and so are listeners. Future opportunities for Air America are impressive. If I am to dream a little more, I envision an affiliation with liberal book publishers, producers of documentaries and independent movies, and other media opportunities.

At the beginning, while we were organizing, we were worried that either Clear Channel or Infinity would pick up on this obvious market and start their own lineup of liberal talk show hosts. They could have easily done this as owners of a number of stations in each major city. But they didn't because they did not believe that there was a market out there.

So where did all those liberals come from? All the best selling political documentaries are liberal. Michael Moore has broken all records with his documentary *Fahrenheit 911* from this so-called non-existent audience. Publishers are looking for all kinds of revealing, anti-establishment books. There is a new flurry of people of like minds who now know they have company in their dissatisfaction with where the country has gone in recent years. With this new media revolution, voters who feel disenfranchised by the swing of the country to the far right, now have a voice that speaks for them. Now that is what I call a great emerging market.

Postscript

Henry A. Wallace, Vice President from 1941-1945 wrote a piece in The New York Times on April 9, 1944, called *The Danger of American Fascism.* It is as timely today as it was when it was written. I include it because it is such a clear argument—not to mention prescient—for the cause of diversity in the media. He wrote:

> The dangerous American fascist is the man who wants to do in the United States in an American way what Hitler did in Germany in a Prussian way. The American fascist would prefer not to use violence. His method is to poison the channels of public information. With a fascist the problem is never how best to present the truth to the public but how best to use the news to deceive the public into giving the fascist and his group more money or more power.

> …If we define an American fascist as one who in case of conflict puts money and power ahead of human beings, then there are undoubtedly several million fascists in the United States. There are probably several hundred thousand if we narrow the definition to include only those who in their search for money and power are ruthless and deceitful. Most

American fascists are enthusiastically supporting the war effort. They are doing this even in those cases where they hope to have profitable connections with German chemical firms after the war ends. They are patriotic in time of war because it is to their interest to be so, but in time of peace they follow power and the dollar wherever they may lead."

The American fascists are most easily recognized by their deliberate perversion of truth and fact. Their newspapers and propaganda carefully cultivate every fissure of disunity, every crack in the common front against fascism. They use every opportunity to impugn democracy. They use isolationism as a slogan to conceal their own selfish imperialism. They cultivate hate and distrust of both Britain and Russia. They claim to be super-patriots, but they would destroy every liberty guaranteed by the Constitution. They demand free enterprise, but are the spokesmen for monopoly and vested interest. Their final objective toward which all their deceit is directed is to capture political power so that, using the power of the state and the power of the market simultaneously, they may keep the common man in eternal subjection.

As I suggested earlier in this book, the post Second World War period may have been quite different if Henry Wallace had been nominated as Vice President instead of Harry Truman. Although the media has painted Truman as a sort of folk hero, the reality is he was unprepared to be President in that critical period. Truman, I believe, was incapable of addressing the larger human issues because he had to capitulate to power, money, and the entrenched bureaucracy including the military establishment. Not much has changed since then, except the fact that the domination of the corporate owned media is poisoning our minds to a point that—we can only hope—it may unwittingly be causing its own demise.

The Southern and extreme fundamentalist wing of the Republican Party is exactly what Wallace described as American fascists in his *New York Times* piece of 1944. Yet today, any mention or comparison to fascists is used as an excuse to "accuse the accusers."

What is the objective truth about these people, for those who are not afraid to say it? The Southern strategy of the Republican Party is based upon racism and fundamentalism. Why else would Bush pander to that wing of the Party by speaking at Bob Jones University, fund faith-based initiatives contrary to our Constitution, ban all medical and health procedures that have the hint of conflicting with a fundamentalist interpretation of the bible, and pepper his speeches with apocalyptic language? Yet the press chooses to continue to marginalize those who claim this is anti-democratic and in contradiction to the Constitution of the United States.

The press is complicit, along with the Republican majority who, together in silence, refuse to reject the destructive wing of their Party. It is my hope that the road to Air America will grow into a network of superhighways that will bring the necessary information to our people, and honesty back to our public discourse. I know Charles Drobny would have felt the same way.

Appendix A

$\mathbf{H}$ere's proof positive that if you get your news from Fox News Channel, you get fed a bunch of lies—

In the autumn of 2003 I was interviewed by Byron York, White House correspondent for the *National Review*, the preeminent conservative magazine in America. In his story he made reference to an essay I wrote, entitled "The Vast Right Wing Conspiracy," in which I made mention of the long-standing (1926–1942, several months *after* the declaration of war) business relationship between President George W. Bush's grandfather Prescott and the Nazi regime in Germany.

In that article, and a subsequent interview with Brit Hume on the Fox News Channel, York took my information about Prescott Bush and slyly marginalized it by claiming it was unsubstantiated. In the Fox interview, York and Hume went even further by taking great pains to link me—through my assertions about Prescott Bush—to perennial fringe figure Lyndon LaRouche (a man who, in many ways, stands to the right of Patrick Buchannan).

What follows is my letter to the editor of the *National Review*, as well as two solid sources for my information on Prescott Bush.

Sheldon Drobny's message to the editor of *National Review*

October 25, 2003

Yesterday I had a very cordial conversation with Byron York about his article and guest appearance on Brit Hume's Special Report. I told Byron that I generally do not give political interviews to either left or right wing media. However, I agreed to speak to Byron a few weeks ago. In the main, I do not agree with the positions taken by your magazine. However, I recognize that the *National Review* is a respected conservative publication. So I agreed to give Byron the interview.

Byron accurately described me as a venture capitalist and philanthropist in his piece. He also researched my writings on the web site called Makethemaccountable.com. I am a student of history and enjoy researching what I call lost history. If you read the articles I wrote objectively, I have written about unknown points of history in the 20th century. I have criticized both Democrat and Republican presidents. I criticized Wilson for sending troops to attack the Soviet Union in 1918 (T. Roosevelt and the Republicans did as well). I criticized both the Bush and Clinton Administrations for missing an opportunity to positively change those countries under Soviet dominance after the collapse of the Soviet Union.

However, in one article I wrote, *The Vast Right Wing Conspiracy,* I made the following comment:

"Nazi Germany's military industrial complex allowed it to rearm and start a second world war. Much of the support for Germany's rearmament came from American and international businesses, a scandal that has never been completely made public. Very few Americans know that Prescott Bush, our president's grandfather, supplied Nazi Germany with such assistance. He did not stop until President Roosevelt, in 1942 froze some of his assets under the Trading With

The Enemies Act. The information is documented, but is not known by most Americans because, as in any successful fascist regime, the press is prevented from publishing it."

The theme of the article was to give the reader a prospective of what "fascism" or "corporatism" mean in the context of modern nonracial economic and political terms. It was written in January of this year on a web site that surely has little influence on political discourse in this country. In other words, I write as a hobby and have never attempted to be in the "limelight." Byron asked me if I believed the Prescott Bush story. I told him to go to GOOGLE and search BUSH NAZI himself. I got over 400,000 hits. One of them was the quote he used in his article written by the alleged LaRouche follower. However, there were many credible sources he could have used in his article including the most recent articles written in the AP and *New Hampshire Journal.*

I have enclosed the article by Mr. Buchanan written recently after release of information from the National Archives about Bush, Harriman and other industrialists who traded with the Nazis. I did not accuse our President of being a Nazi nor did I blame him for his fathers deeds. Fascism, as a political and economic commentary, is not Nazism. My criticism of our President concerning preemptive war is very much in line with main stream conservative thinking.

Both my parents were immigrants from Poland. My uncle, Chaim Lopata, was a documented hero of the Warsaw Ghetto Uprising in 1943. I have honored him with a chaired professorship at the University of Illinois Jewish Studies Program. My commentary about the American industrialists who traded with Nazis is especially relevant to me. The "Dark Angel" that York referred about is not me, but Prescott Bush and those who participated with him. It is their shame, not mine, that is a horrible legacy to our great country.

Sheldon Drobny
Chairman
Paradigm Group, LLC

New Hampshire Gazette

The long-rumored connection between the Bush family and the Nazis has been confirmed with documents from the National Archives. We had it first. The AP checked it out, and put their version of the story on the wire Friday. At our last count 25 outfits had run it, including *Newsday* (NY); *The Atlanta Journal-Constitution* (GA); *The Washington* (DC) *Times; The Fort Worth* (TX) *Star Telegram; The Kansas City* (MO) *Star; The Times Picayune* (LA); *and The Stamford* (CT) *Advocate.*

Bush–Nazi Link Confirmed

By John Buchanan
from *The New Hampshire Gazette,* Vol. 248, No. 1,
October 10, 2003

WASHINGTON—After 60 years of inattention and even denial by the U.S. media, newly-uncovered government documents in The National Archives and Library of Congress reveal that Prescott Bush, the grandfather of President George W. Bush, served as a business partner of and U.S. banking operative for the financial architect of the Nazi war machine from 1926 until 1942, when Congress took aggressive action against Bush and his "enemy national" partners.

The documents also show that Bush and his colleagues, according to reports from the U.S. Department of the Treasury and FBI, tried to conceal their financial alliance with German industrialist Fritz Thyssen, a steel and coal baron who, beginning in the mid-1920s, personally funded Adolf Hitler's rise to power by the subversion of democratic principle and German law.

Furthermore, the declassified records demonstrate that Bush and his associates, who included E. Roland Harriman, younger brother of American icon W. Averell Harriman, and George Herbert Walker, President Bush's maternal great-grandfather, continued their dealings with the German industrial baron for nearly eight months after the U.S. entered the war.

No Story?

For six decades these historical facts have gone unreported by the mainstream U.S. media. The essential facts have appeared on the Internet and in relatively obscure books, but were dismissed by the media and Bush family as undocumented diatribes. This story has also escaped the attention of "official" Bush biographers, Presidential historians and publishers of U.S. history books covering World War II and its aftermath...

Associated Press

Bush Ancestor's Bank Seized by Gov't

Fri., Oct. 17, 7:25 P.M. ET
By Jonathan D. Salant, Associated Press Writer

WASHINGTON—President Bush's grandfather was a director of a bank seized by the federal government because of its ties to a German industrialist who helped bankroll Adolf Hitler's rise to power, government documents show.

Prescott Bush was one of seven directors of Union Banking Corp., a New York investment bank owned by a bank controlled by the Thyssen family, according to recently declassified National Archives documents reviewed by The Associated Press.

Fritz Thyssen was an early financial supporter of Hitler, whose Nazi party Thyssen believed was preferable to communism. The documents do not show any evidence Bush directly aided that effort. His position with Union Banking never was a political issue for Bush, who was elected to the Senate from Connecticut in 1952.

Reports of Bush's involvement with the seized bank have been circulating on the Internet for years and have been reported by some mainstream media. The newly declassified documents provide additional details about the Union Banking–Thyssen connection ...

Appendix B

Published on Tuesday, December 3, 2002, by CommonDreams.org

Talking Back To Talk Radio—
Fairness, Democracy, and Profits

by Thom Hartmann

"All Democrats are fat, lazy, and stupid," the talk-show host said in grave, serious tones as if he were uttering a sacred truth.

We were driving to Michigan for the holidays, and I was tuning around, listening for the stations I'd worked for two and three decades ago. I turned the dial. "It's a Hannity For Humanity house," a different host said, adding that the Habitat For Humanity home he'd apparently hijacked for his own self-promotion would only be given to a family that swears it's conservative. "No liberals are going to get this house," he said.

Turning the dial again, we found a convicted felon ranting about the importance of government having ever-more powers to monitor, investigate, and prosecute American citizens without having to worry about constitutional human rights protections. Apparently the combining of nationwide German police agencies (following the terrorist attack of February 1933 when the Parliament building was set afire) into one giant Fatherland Security Agency answerable only to the Executive Branch, the Reichssicherheitshauptamt and its SchutzStaffel, was a lesson of history this guy had completely forgotten. Neither, apparently, do most Americans recall that the single most powerful device used to bring about the SS and its political master was radio.

Is history repeating itself?

Setting aside the shrill and nonsensical efforts of those who suggest the corporate-owned media in America is "liberal," the situation with regard to talk radio is particularly perplexing: It doesn't even carry a pretense of political balance. While the often-understated Al Gore recently came right out and said that much of the corporate-owned media are "part and parcel of the Republican Party," those who listen to talk radio know it has swung so far to the right that even Dwight Eisenhower or Barry Goldwater would be shocked.

Average Americans across the nation are wondering how could it be that a small fringe of the extreme right has so captured the nation's airwaves? And done it in such an effective fashion that when they attack folks like Tom Daschle, he and his family actually get increased numbers of death threats? How is it that ex-felons like John Poindexter's protégé Ollie North and Nixon's former burglar G. Gordon Liddy have become stars? How is it that ideologues like Rush Limbaugh can openly promote hard-right Republicans, and avoid a return of the dead-since-Reagan Fairness Doctrine (and get around the desire of the American public for fairness) by claiming what they do is "just entertainment"?

And, given the domination of talk radio by the fringe hard-right that represents the political views of only a small segment of America, why is it that the vast majority of talk radio stations across the nation never run even an occasional centrist or progressive show in the midst of their all-right, all-the-time programming day?

Even within the radio industry itself, there's astonishment.

Program directors and station managers I've talked with claim they have to program only hard-right hosts. They point out that when they insert even a few hours of a centrist or progressive talk host into a typical talk-radio day, the station's phone lines light up with angry, flaming reactions from listeners; even advertisers get calls of protest. Just last month, a talk-radio station manager told me solemnly, "Only right-wingers listen to AM radio any more. The lefties would rather read."

How could this be? After all, an "environmentalist" Democrat — Al Gore—won the majority of the popular vote in the last presidential election, with a half-million more votes than any other presidential candidate (of any party) in the entire history of the nation. How could it be that there are only two Democratic or progressive voices in major national radio syndication, and only a small handful in partial syndication or on local shows?

The issue is important for two reasons.

First, in a nation that considers itself a democratic republic, the institutions of democracy are imperiled by a lack of balanced national debate on issues of critical importance. As both Nazi Germany and Stalinist Russia learned, a steady radio drumbeat of a single viewpoint—from either end of the political spectrum—is not healthy for democracy when opposing voices are marginalized.

Second, what's happened recently in the radio industry represents a business opportunity of significant proportions. The station manager I talked with is wrong, because of something in science known as "sample bias." He was assuming his radio listeners represent all radio listeners, a critical error.

Here's why the talk radio scene is so dominated by the right, and how it can become more democratic. First, a very brief history:

When radio first became a national force in the 1920s and 1930s, most stations programmed everything. Country/Western music would be followed by Big Band, followed by Mozart, followed by drama or comedy. Everything was jumbled together, and people need-ed the newspaper program guides to know when to listen to what.

As the market matured, and drama and comedy moved to televi-sion, radio stations realized there were specific market segments and niches within those segments to which they could program. And they realized that people within those niches had very specific tastes. Country/Western listeners only wanted to hear Country/Western—Big Band put them off, and classical music put them to sleep. Classical music fans, on the other hand, became irri-tated when Country/Western or the early versions of Rock 'n Roll came on the air. And Rock fans clicked off the moment Frank Sinatra came on.

So, as those of us who've worked in the business saw, stations began to program into these specific musical niches, and it led to a new renaissance (and profit windfall) in the radio business.

But to make money in the new world of radio that emerged in the 1950s, you had to be true to your niche.

When I was a Country/Western DJ, if I had tried to drop in a song from The Rolling Stones, my listeners would have gone bal-listic, calling in and angrily complaining. Similarly, when I was doing morning drive-time Rock, it would have been suicide to drop in four minutes of Mozart. Smart programmers know to always hold true to their niche and their listeners.

At first, radio talk shows were seen as a way of fulfilling FCC community service requirements. In the late 1960s and early 1970s, when I was a reporter and news anchor at WITL-AM/FM in Lansing, Michigan, we had an afternoon talk show that ran from 2 to 3 P.M. Usually hosted by the station's general manager, the late Chuck Drake, and sometimes fill-in hosted by us in the news staff, the show was overtly run to satisfy the FCC's mandate that stations "serve the public interest." Thus, our talk show focused mostly on public-interest issues, from local and national politics to lost dog reports, and we tried hard to present all viewpoints fairly (as was then required by the FCC's Fairness Doctrine).

In that, we were following a long radio tradition. Modern talk radio as a major force in America started in 1926, when Catholic priest Father Charles E. Coughlin took to the airwaves. By the mid-1930s, as many as a full third of the entire nation—an estimated 45 million people—listened to his weekly broadcasts. His downfall, and the end of the fifteen-year era of talk radio he'd both created and dominated, came in the early 1940s when the nation was at war and Hitler was shipping millions of Jews to the death camps. For reasons still unknown (Alzheimer's is suspected), Coughlin launched into hard-right anti-Semitic tirades in his broadcasts, blaming an international Jewish conspiracy for communism, the Great Depression, World War II, and most of the world's other ills. His sudden shift to the radical right disgusted his listeners, and led his superiors in the Catholic Church to demand he retire from radio and return to his parish duties where he died in relative obscurity. Many say the Fairness Doctrine came about in part because of Coughlin.

A generation later, a new Father Coughlin emerged in the form of Rush Limbaugh, an articulate and talented talk-show host out of Sacramento. Joe Pyne (a conservative who almost always had a liberal with him on the air) was dead, and conservative investors and programmers were looking to unseat the fabulously popular liberal talker Alan Berg and bring "balance" to America's airwaves. (In June of 1984, the year Rush began "issues talk" on Sacramento's KFBK, Berg was machine-gunned to death by right-wingers claiming they were from the Aryan Nation.) Within four years, Rush rose to national status by offering his program free of charge to stations across the nation. Station managers, not being business dummies, laid off local talent and picked up Rush's free show, leading to a national phenomena: the Limbaugh show was one of America's greatest radio success stories, spreading from state to state faster than any modern talk show had ever done. (Such free or barter offerings are now standard in the industry.)

And, station managers discovered, there is a loyal group of radio listeners (around 20 million occasional listeners, with perhaps one to five million who consider themselves "dittoheads") who embraced Rush's brand of overt hard-right spin, believing every word he says even though he claims his show is "just entertainment" to avoid a reemergence of the Fairness Doctrine and the political-activity provisions of McCain/Feingold. The sudden success of Rush led local radio station programmers to look for more of the same: there was a sudden demand for Rush-clone talkers who could meet the needs of the nation's Rush-bonded listeners, and the all-right-wing-talk radio format emerged, dominated by Limbaugh and Limbaugh-clones in both style and political viewpoint.

Thus, the extreme fringe of the right wing dominates talk radio not because all radio listeners are right-wingers, but, instead, because the right wingers and their investors were the first to the market with a consistent and predictable programming slant, making right-wing-talk the first large niche to mature in the newly emergent talk segment of the radio industry. Listeners always know what they'll get with Rush or one of his clones, and programming to a loyal and identifiable audience is both the dream and the necessity of every radio station's management.

Which brings us to the opportunity this represents for Democrats, progressives, radio stations, and those interested in supporting democracy by bringing balance to the nation's airwaves.

Going back to the music radio programming analogy, think of Rush and Rush-clone-right-wing-talk as if it were Country/Western music. It's unique, instantly recognizable, and has a loyal and definable audience, just like any of the specific music niches. This explains why it's nearly impossible to successfully program progressive talk in the halfway fashion that's often been tried (and often failed) up to today.

The rules are the same as in music programming: any competent radio station program director knows they'll get angry listeners if they drop an hour of Rock or Rap into a Country/Western programming day. It's equally easy to predict that if you were to drop an hour or three of a progressive talker like Mike Malloy or Peter

Werbe into a day dominated by Rush and his clones, the listeners will be outraged. After all, those particular listeners thought they were tuned into an all-right-wing station.

But that response doesn't mean—as conservatives in the radio industry suggest—that there is no market for progressive talk radio. What it means is that there's not yet an awakening in the broadcast industry to the reality that they're missing a huge unserved market. But, like with right-wing talk, for balanced or progressive talk radio to succeed it must be programmed consistently throughout the day (and with talent as outrageous and interesting as Rush and his most successful clones).

Most stations who today identify themselves as "talk radio" stations are really programming the specific niche of "hard-right-Republican-talk-radio," and the niche of "progressive-and-Democratic-talk-radio" (which would speak to an equal sized market) is just beginning to emerge and mature. Only a small handful of stations have made a serious effort to program progressive talk, and the only national network to offer any of it in a serious fashion, the "i.e. America Network," hasn't yet made the distinction between "progressive talk" and "soft/advice talk," and, thus, doesn't offer a full day and night's lineup of "hard" progressive talkers along with their "soft" talkers who break up the day.

The key to success for both radio stations and networks is to realize that talk radio isn't a monolithic niche—it's matured into a category, like music did in the 1950s—and within that category there are multiple niches, including the very large demographic niches of conservative talk, relationship-advice talk, progressive talk, and sports talk, and smaller niches of travel talk, investment talk, medical talk, local talk, etc.

The station programmers I've talked with who've tried a progressive or centrist talker for an hour or two, only to get angry responses from dittoheads, think this means only extreme-right-wing talkers (and, ideally, convicted felons or those who "declare war on liberals") will make money for their station. And, because they've already carved out the hard-right-Republican-talk niche and alienated the progressive/Democrat niche, they're right.

But for stations who want to get into talk in a market already dominated by right-wing talkers on competing stations, the irrefutable evidence of national elections and polls shows that believing only right-wingers will bring listeners (and advertisers) is a mistake. All they need do is what anybody with music programming experience would recommend: identify their niche and stick with it. (Cynics say stations won't program Democrats because owners and management are all "rich Republicans": to this, I say they should listen to some of the music being profitably produced and programmed by America's largest publishing and broadcasting corporations. Profits, for better or worse, are relatively opinion-free.)

By running Democratic/progressive-talk in a programming day free of right-wing talkers, stations will open up a new niche and ride it to success. This is a particularly huge opportunity for music stations who look with envy at the success of talk stations in their market, but haven't been willing to jump in because all the best right-wing talkers are already on the competition: all they need do is put on progressive talkers, and they'll open a new, unserved, and profitable niche.

And, with right-wing ideologues now in charge of our government, the time has never been better: as Rush showed during the Clinton years (the peak of his success), "issues" talk thrives best in an underdog environment. It's in the American psyche to give a fair listen to people challenging the party in power.

Those stations that take the plunge into progressive talk will serve democracy by offering a loyal opposition (which Americans always appreciate), and earn healthy revenues in an industry where it's increasingly difficult to find a profitable niche. And whichever network is first to realize this simple reality and provide stations with solid progressive or Democrat talk programming will build a strong, viable, and financially healthy business.

If you're in the business, consider seriously this advice from an old radio station programmer. And if you listen to radio, call your local stations (both talk and music) to let them know that you want to hear progressive or Democrat voices, and will even patronize the advertisers of such shows when they run them.

It's time to revitalize democracy and rational political discourse by returning balance to our nation's airwaves, and the profits to be made in this huge unfilled niche may be just the catalyst to bring it about.

Thom Hartmann is the author of *Unequal Protection: The Rise of Corporate Dominance and the Theft of Human Rights*—http://www. unequalprotection.com/ and http://www.thomhartmann.com/. Permission is granted to reprint this article in print or web media, so long as this credit is attached.

Appendix C

Radio Daze—Inside Air America's Troubles Optimism and Shaky Finances

In an Election Year, Talk Radio for Liberals Made Sense; A $24 Million Shortfall

Al Franken's Kitchen Surprise

Julia Angwin and Sarah McBride

On March 30, the night before Air America went on the air, the liberal radio network threw itself a $70,000 party at Manhattan's hip Maritime Hotel. More than 1,000 guests, including Yoko Ono and Tim Robbins, drank red, white and blue vodka cocktails as they toasted the network's bid to challenge the dominance of conservative talk radio.

But behind the scenes, Air America was running out of money. Today several employees say they still haven't been reimbursed for the costs of attending the New York launch. "It was a fun party, until I knew I was paying for it," says Bob Visotcky, Air America's former Los Angeles market manager, who hasn't been reimbursed for his hotel room and flight.

131

Mr. Visotcky wasn't the only insider in the dark about the company's problems. Many of Air America's investors and executives say they thought the network had raised more than $30 million, based on assurances from its owners, Guam-based entrepreneurs Evan M. Cohen and Rex Sorensen. In fact, Air America had raised only $6 million, Mr. Cohen concedes. Within six weeks of the launch, those funds had been spent and the company owed creditors more than $2 million.

When the problems came to light, "we realized that we had all been duped," says David Goodfriend, the company's acting chief operating officer. Messrs. Cohen and Sorensen say they didn't mislead anyone about the company's finances. They say they planned to invest more over time but didn't because of cultural differences with other managers. Both resigned in early May.

Five months before a presidential election, Air America should be on a roll. Instead, it's grappling with a financial crisis. Creditors are lined up at the door, and it is off the air in two big markets, Los Angeles and Chicago.

Air America's left-leaning orientation gave the fledgling network a public profile and helped lure donors, including RealNetworks Inc.'s Chief Executive Rob Glaser and New York's Durst family of real-estate developers. It also helped attract big-name talent, including comedian Al Franken. Amid the hype, however, investors and executives overlooked Air America's haphazard organization, opaque finances and flawed business strategy.

Trying to make a big political splash, Air America embarked on an ambitious and costly plan to get radio-station owners to carry the network's entire 24-hour lineup. Typically, networks allow stations to pick the shows they want, and both sides share the advertising revenue. Air America got its way in smaller markets. In big cities, Air America agreed to pay for airtime, which ultimately cost more than it could afford.

"When you believe you're doing work for the greater good, you don't question as much," says Javier Saade, a former Air America executive vice president. "People never questioned the curves and obstacles on the road. People just said, 'We're on the road.'"

Company executives now say the business is stabilizing. They note that the network's early ratings have been positive, and its business plan has been restructured. The company has received enough cash from investors to stay afloat, and it is negotiating with its creditors. Air America is "on track" to meet its financial goals, says Doug Kreeger, Air America's current chief executive.

Air America was conceived by a wealthy Chicago couple, Anita and Sheldon Drobny. Mr. Drobny is a venture capitalist and liberal activist who writes an occasional column for a Web site that has compared Republican control of Congress and the White House to the Nazis' rise to power in Germany.

After some unsuccessful fund-raising efforts, the Drobnys met Mr. Cohen in the spring of 2003 through a meeting brokered by Mr. Goodfriend, a former Clinton aide who was interested in the radio concept. Mr. Goodfriend, 36 years old, and Mr. Cohen, 37, attended Beloit College in Wisconsin together.

Mr. Cohen teamed up with Mr. Sorensen, 58, a business partner and the founder of Sorensen Pacific Broadcasting Inc., a network of five radio stations in Guam and Saipan. The two men agreed to buy the concept from the Drobnys for about $1 million, according to four people familiar with the transaction. The Drobnys haven't yet been paid. Messrs. Cohen and Sorensen say payment was based on performance milestones that haven't been met.

In Guam, where he was born, Mr. Cohen was involved in a number of ventures at least some of which were unsuccessful, including a publishing company, an ad agency and a market research firm. He says the businesses were hurt by the Asian economic crisis of the late 1990s.

Joe Calvo, the general manager of Guam's Pacific Telestations Inc., which owns TV and radio stations, says Mr. Cohen's defunct ad agency owes him $20,000. Mark Pangalinan, president of Guam conglomerate M.V. Pangalinan Enterprises, says the same ad company owes his real-estate division four years in rent; it also owes another division several years' worth of employee health-insurance premiums. Mr. Cohen denies owing both companies money. Mr. Goodfriend says he thought Mr. Cohen was a successful businessman and says he was unaware of these disputes.

In October, Mr. Goodfriend introduced Messrs. Cohen and Sorensen to a potential chief executive. Mark Walsh, a 50-year-old former America Online Inc. executive, had run an e-commerce site called Verticalnet Inc., which was briefly one of the highest-flying dot-com stocks with a peak value of $12.4 billion. More recently, Mr. Walsh headed Internet operations for John Kerry's presidential campaign.

Mr. Walsh says he asked Mr. Cohen for proof of his assets. The entrepreneur showed Mr. Walsh documents that Mr. Cohen represented as real-estate and cash holdings valued at millions of dollars, Mr. Walsh says. Mr. Cohen denies saying the assets were his alone. He says the documents combined his assets with those of Mr. Sorensen and another business partner, Brooklyn real-estate developer Charles Cara.

Mr. Walsh says he was impressed by Mr. Cohen's "seductive" account of his battle with cancer. Mr. Cohen told Mr. Walsh and others that he was diagnosed with brain cancer in 2001 only to make a miraculous recovery that spurred him to devote his life to liberal causes. This new radio network, "represented the confluence of business pragmatism and social progressiveness that I wanted for my second chance in life," Mr. Cohen wrote in a fund-raising letter to television journalist Bill Moyers, who didn't invest.

Mr. Walsh became chief executive of a holding company called Progress Media that owned two other entities. One company was set up to create programming and another was designed to buy radio stations.

Air America's purchasing arm struggled to buy radio stations in major markets—where few big stations were interested in turning over their entire airtime to Air America. But most major market stations were too expensive and the network's $36 million credit line hadn't come through. So the network eventually had to sign costly leasing deals to buy airtime. The expense of the leases, which have largely fallen out of favor in the radio industry, helped deplete Air America's operating cash.

Rick Cummings, president of the radio division at Emmis Communications Corp., one of the nation's biggest station owners, had brief talks with Air America. But he didn't want to dedicate an entire station to its shows, as the network requested. "They quickly realized there were a lot of things they didn't know, and one was how to do radio," says Mr. Cummings.

Messrs. Cohen and Sorensen were meanwhile raising money for their programming arm. They told potential backers they would put $12 million of their own money in the venture, according to two investors and Messrs. Walsh and Saade, who attended many pitches. Messrs. Cohen and Sorensen also told investors and employees they had raised $18 million from individual donors, these people say.

Norman Wain, a Cleveland radio entrepreneur, says Mr. Cohen told him that Air America already had $30 million in the bank. Mr. Wain says he was told that his contribution would not be used until a separate round of financing was completed.

Messrs. Walsh and Saade say Mr. Cohen told them that TV producer Norman Lear had given Air America $2 million and pledged another $2 million. They also say Mr. Cohen told them that Laurie David, wife of comedian Larry David, had invested $2 million and pledged another $4 million.

Buoyed by the good news, Mr. Walsh told reporters on a March 11 conference call that the network was "well on our way" to raising "upward of $30 million" by its planned March 31 launch.

In fact, Mr. Lear and Ms. David were approached by Mr. Cohen but didn't invest, their spokespeople say. The amount raised totaled only $6 million, Mr. Cohen and Air America executives agree. Mr. Cohen denies telling Messrs. Walsh and Saade about investments from the two Hollywood bigwigs and denies misleading Mr. Wain and other investors about the fund-raising efforts. He says anyone who thought the deals had gone through were not in the loop.

Mr. Cohen says he told investors and others at the company he would invest "up to $12 million" through a partnership that included himself, his brother, Mr. Sorensen and Mr. Cara, the real-estate developer. Mr. Cohen says they invested more than $1 million in the company and intended to put in more. Mr. Cohen says he told investors and executives that the bulk of the $12 million would come from Mr. Cara.

Mr. Cara says in an interview he was willing to invest up to $12 million but held off when Mr. Cohen ran into problems at the radio network. Mr. Walsh says he doesn't recall Mr. Cohen mentioning Mr. Cara.

Mr. Sorensen, in an e-mail response to questions from a reporter, said: "In all our discussions in private placement documents we listed our LLC with Charlie [Cara] as the funding source being used to further fund the company. This was not hidden in any way."

Meanwhile, the network was starting to create a buzz. Advertising salespeople lined up $700,000 in commitments before the network even started, a former advertising executive at the network says.

The war in Iraq and the pending election had fiercely polarized national politics. Personal animosity toward President Bush seemed as intense as the antipathy once aimed at Bill Clinton, an anger that did much to feed the explosion in conservative radio.

The network's lineup included Mr. Franken, a former *Saturday Night Live* writer and performer turned best-selling author of liberal tomes. Also on board were actress Janeane Garofalo and rapper Chuck D. Air America leased stations in the top three radio markets: New York, Chicago and Los Angeles. Its high-profile launch party gave the network a big publicity boost.

But bills weren't getting paid. Mr. Visotcky, the former Los Angeles market manager, says he discovered in March the company hadn't paid the rent on its office space there. He lost his job later when Air America was kicked off the air in that city. Mr. Cohen says the rent wasn't paid because of a contractual dispute. In April, vendors stopped delivering office supplies because they weren't getting paid and contractors, such as electricians, complained their checks weren't arriving.

One of the network's on-air personalities, Randi Rhodes, formerly of WJNO in West Palm Beach, Fla., opened her own checkbook when her staff wasn't paid. Ms. Rhodes says she found "a group that was running the place that was absolutely not up to it." The New York studio had no air conditioning and some technical equipment didn't work. In its first few days, the network sometimes sputtered off the air.

Mr. Cohen concedes the company should have had tighter financial controls and blames the cash crunch on perks such as car services. Mr. Sorensen says he's "not aware of any bill over 60 days [past due] or any employee whose payroll was not immediately dealt with, if there was an issue."

Mr. Walsh says Mr. Sorensen, who was acting chief financial officer, and Mr. Cohen, who was chairman, wouldn't give him control of the checkbook or allow him a look at the financial books. Messrs. Cohen and Sorensen say Mr. Walsh had access to the company's financial documents.

When he returned home to Washington after the launch, Mr. Walsh left a voicemail for Mr. Cohen criticizing the company's lax financial controls and poor organization. Mr. Cohen responded in a three-page letter, dated April 7: "I had expected you to be in constant, close contact with Rex & me, discern what our priorities were, take on the 'family business' culture that we have used successfully in the past, and execute accordingly," Mr. Cohen wrote. "For whatever reason, and it really doesn't matter why, that just did not happen."

Unable to resolve their differences, Mr. Walsh quit on April 12, but his departure wasn't announced for a few weeks. Mr. Goodfriend, who had been the company's legal counsel, was named acting chief operating officer. Mr. Cohen took on the responsibilities of CEO.

At that time, Air America's leasing deals in Los Angeles and Chicago began to fall apart. Air America had bought time on KBLA and WNTD from MultiCultural Radio Broadcasting Inc. but the two companies battled over interpretation of the contract.

The dispute boiled over when MultiCultural locked Air America out of its studios and kicked it off the airwaves in Chicago and Los Angeles. An Air America employee wrote on the network's Web site that MultiCultural's Chief Executive Arthur Liu was a "Liu-ser" and "Liu- cifer" and that Air America was "chasing him down with a pipe wrench."

Air America sued in New York Supreme Court and a judge ordered MultiCultural to put it back on the air in Chicago, where Air America had made more payments, through April, but not in Los Angeles. After that ruling expired, the two companies couldn't come to terms and Air America was off the air in both cities.

As the network tried to repair the damage, it was also fighting with Mr. Franken over how his salary was paid. As the network's star, Mr. Franken had negotiated a pay package valued at more than $1 million a year, according to a copy of the contract viewed by *The Wall Street Journal.* On the evening of April 26 Mr. Goodfriend says he was asked by Mr. Cohen to show Mr. Franken a deposit slip that would prove he'd been paid a portion of his salary. Mr. Cohen says he only asked Mr. Goodfriend to negotiate with Mr. Franken.

The next day, Mr. Goodfriend went to Mr. Franken's Manhattan apartment to meet Mr. Franken's wife, who manages her husband's finances. Over the Frankens' kitchen table, the two tore open an envelope sent over by Mr. Cohen that they thought was going to contain proof of the payment. All they found was a stack of irrelevant documents.

Mr. Goodfriend, who had no access to the company's finances, says he had previously chalked up the network's snafus to growing pains. Now, he worried that Air America had less money than he thought. Mr. Goodfriend started investigating and called an emergency telephone board meeting to quiz Messrs. Cohen and Sorensen about Mr. Franken's salary and other financial issues. Mr. Goodfriend had an outside attorney listen in.

Over the next few days, the pair from Guam talked to company lawyers, executives and investors. After hearing what they considered unsatisfactory answers, the investors called a meeting on May 5 at Air America's Park Avenue headquarters. They asked Messrs. Cohen and Sorensen to resign and hand over voting control of their shares to Mr. Goodfriend, according to three people familiar with the negotiations.

After the meeting, Air America executives examined the company's finances. "When we finally gained access to the bank accounts, we realized they were empty," Mr. Saade says. Mr. Cohen denies the bank accounts were empty although he concedes there wasn't much money left.

Messrs. Cohen and Sorensen say they were asked to resign because of cultural differences with other managers. Neither would be more specific. "There was no longer any support for Rex and I, so as investors, why would we continue to go forward?" Mr. Cohen says. He adds they deserve credit for their efforts. "We built something from nothing," he says.

Mr. Goodfriend, who says he was exhausted by the turmoil, also resigned but agreed to stay until the end of May.

Air America's investors created a new company, Piquant LLC, which bought the assets of the old company, named a new CEO and simplified its business plan. Rather than buying stations or leasing time, Air America is following a more conventional route, allowing local stations to pick up portions of the lineup. It's on the air in New York and fourteen other markets including Portland, Ore., and Chapel Hill, N.C.

In a startup, says Mr. Franken, people often exaggerate what they have. Mr. Cohen, he says, "did just that, and somehow got us on the air. For that, I guess I owe him some gratitude."

Julia Angwin and Sarah McBride, "Radio Daze—Inside Air America's Troubles Optimism and Shaky Finances," *The Wall Street Journal,* Monday, June 21, 2004,

Glossary of New Orwellian Terms

---

1. Spin = lie
2. War on terrorists = Perpetual war for the benefit of the rich corporations
3. Patriot act = Code for freedom is not patriotic
4. Quid pro quo = Bribe
5. The death tax = Keep the rich families rich
6. Reducing taxes increases the surplus = $2+2=5$
7. Federal tax cuts benefit everyone = State sales tax and real estate tax increases will kill the middle class
8. Compassionate conservative = We feel sorry for you but no help is coming
9. Republican southern strategy = racism works
10. Deregulation = Regulation to benefit big corporations and crush competition
11. Free market = Consolidation increasing barriers to compete
12. Accurate reporting = Out of context skewing of facts
13. Spending = Everything except military spending
14. The defense budget = R&D subsidies for the arms industry
15. Conservative = A good person who believes his or her ideas are best for the country
16. Liberal = An evil person who supports government giveaways and is soft on defense
17. Globalization = A process in which multinational corporations benefit at the expense of the workers and middle class.